UNLEASH YOUR INNER WOLF

REACHING APEX-LEVEL MASTERY IN LIFE, BUSINESS, AND DIGITAL MARKETING

MAOR BENAIM

THE WOLF MARKETING, LTD

To the fearless souls who dare to explore the wilderness of entrepreneurship in digital marketing and reach apex level in business, my dedicated readers and fellow adventurers,

I extend my heartfelt gratitude to you for embarking on this transformative expedition alongside me. Your unwavering support and insatiable curiosity serve as the driving force behind the wisdom and insights woven into the fabric of these pages.

May "Unleash Your Inner Wolf" serve as a guiding light, illuminating the path to mastery in business, life and the digital marketing realm, while nurturing the entrepreneurial spirit within you. Within these chapters, may you discover not just knowledge and inspiration, but the potent alchemy that transforms dreams into reality.

With profound appreciation,

Maor

INTRODUCTION

In the wild there are two kinds of animals, there are predators and there is prey.

You either eat or get eaten, and guess what? Business reflects what happens in the wild.

In this book, I'm going to show you how to stop being the fucking prey, even if you are not even aware that you are.

We're going to learn how to create more situations where you become the hunter. Then we're going to raise the stakes and talk about how to move on to becoming an apex predator.

This is all about how you're going to unleash your inner wolf and become a top performer so you can:

- Have better positioning in any deal in the digital marketing world and also in other businesses.
- Choose better partnerships and maintain them.
- Negotiate better deals.
- Identify people trying to make you their prey.
- Get more deals, more easily.
- Choose where to invest your time and money to maximize your return on investment (ROI).

- Dominate any mastermind, conference, or event you'll attend.
- Change your mindset to better see opportunities and become a deal-hunter where you're closing deals and dominating them.

<u>Why This Book?</u>

I'm writing this book because I want to impact as many people as possible by giving them the tools to succeed in entrepreneurship, business, and life, drawing from the lessons I've learned. By reading this book, you'll save yourself a great deal of money, time, and disappointment...but more importantly, and even better, you'll create a better life from both a business and personal perspective.

This book is your shortcut, even if you're not in digital marketing, because it includes lessons and experiences I have learned throughout my years in therapy, coaching and business.

When I started writing this book, it started as a niche book. I wanted to call it "How to Negotiate a Deal in the Affiliate Marketing Space" or something like that. While writing this book, it became the place where I wrote down all of the things I wish someone told me when I first became an entrepreneur, and trying to achieve something even greater than that—a legacy I would want to be remembered by. For me that purpose is helping as many people as possible reach their absolute best, to reach apex level in business and life.

I had two main goals when I approached writing this book.

First that it would be evergreen, as I wanted it to last, with timeless knowledge and wisdom. I wanted people to be able to pick it up even 10 years after I published it and still get value from it. Unlike strategic marketing methods that come and go, algorithms that change, and topics that I usually talk about when I'm invited to speak at events, the strategies in this book are based on a much more solid foundation: my career, my experience, the money I've made, and the money I've lost...turning losses into lessons learned and future wins.

The second would be that it would touch, educate, and help all types of people—a wide audience. While my technical knowledge base usually appeals to more experienced players in the field, this book should speak to everyone—from amateurs who are considering entering the digital marketing space and entrepreneurship in general, to people who are already in the industry—and it would concentrate all of what I've learned through my experience, especially what I've learned spending money, losing money, and making money.

Throughout the year, when I told others that I was writing a book, the majority of people told me I needed to have a backend, I had to sell something at the back end of this book, and I really didn't want to include that because I wanted to keep this book authentic. Also, I do believe that when you spread knowledge and give of yourself, things come your way at the end, even if they take more time.

All while telling my own personal story.

Some parts of this book are meant to be read in order, but most of it could be read by just choosing the chapter you like or feel relates to you. In some chapters I share true stories from my digital marketing career, although even the chapters that do not have personal stories were written based on what I have experienced firsthand. If used skillfully, these stories can save and make you a lot of money and help you more easily navigate the storms that are an inevitable part of business (and even help you come out stronger in some cases).

I really feel like the word "shortcut" has gotten a bad reputation. People on one hand try to avoid taking shortcuts in their careers and a lot understand that there are few, if any, shortcuts when it comes to relationships. There is no good or bad that's absolute. There would always be a way to use that word in a good way, regardless of what branding that word has, and whether you believe it or want to admit it—everyone would love a good shortcut that does not come at any real expense but is based on knowledge.

I really don't believe in shortcuts in life, especially not as a way of living, and never saw it as a sustainable strategy. The only shortcuts in life could be made through other people's experience and advice, hence why the consulting industry is so big, and this is the only way to advance in science and medicine and even art, from songs to painting, there are shortcuts based on what other artists have done, with a different twist. We shouldn't be constantly reinventing the wheel.

This book is your guide to successfully cut through the wild that's out there, your map to avoid becoming the prey and moving up to being an apex leader.

And if I don't manage to change the way you look at business or your mindset after reading the first five chapters then I didn't do my job right. If I do, then you'll have the right mindset to help you overcome many of the obstacles we encounter in business and specifically in the digital marketing industry.

If you're looking for a book for people who are at the earliest stages of their digital marketing understanding, a book that teaches the terminology of this industry, this is not the right book for you.

Importantly, this book is going to help you:

1. Find the RIGHT partner faster and maintain a positive relationship with him, her, or them.
2. Avoid wasting money and time on bad relationships.
3. Set up the right expectations when it comes to the road ahead in the digital marketing space.
4. Planning how to scale yourself and your business, which I cover in the first part of this book.
5. Later in the book we'll talk about how to understand how to filter out the right information and knowledge you should consume.

6. Dive deeper into how to get the most out of every second you're in a conference or a mastermind in the chapters focused on events.
7. Improve your communication skills with strong writing, how not to approach communication, and best practices when it comes to texting, emailing, and calling people you want to recruit as clients or go on calls with.
8. Build a better brand for yourself and become more memorable while giving up fears.
9. Manage relationships with affiliate networks, agency clients and advertisers.
10. Get the highest payout possible in every deal and stabilizing the relationship.
11. Understand the bases of how the platforms work and finding creative ways to manipulate them.

I'm honestly excited for you, if only 30% of the stuff you're about to read in the next few hours would be relevant and implemented by you. This can be a game changer, and it'll make me so happy to see you learn and grow from it, to hear about your experiences when you put these ideas into practice.

The lessons I learned from five personal development couches, 38 psychiatrists, and more than 10 years in entrepreneurship generating over $100 million dollars.

Ready to reach apex status at the top of your game? Let's fucking go.

ONE

THE TRUTH ABOUT AFFILIATE MARKETING AND DIGITAL MARKETING – REALITY VS IMAGINATION

Affiliate marketing, like a lot of things nowadays, became viral and took off when many people in the industry were either actually running affiliate offers and posting about their lives or when courses by real and fake "gurus" or teachers started spreading and were heavily advertised. Since then, it really has become a jungle. Without good navigation or a trustworthy guide, you can take one wrong step and find yourself caught in a trap.

In any case—either by direct intent or not—the dream that was sold to people was the "passive income" dream, work from anywhere, "just a few clicks and start generating money," "on-the-go" easily, no clients to manage, buy your dream car (usually a limo for some reason), travel the world and most likely also leave your 9 to 5 job day job, work only for yourself... In other words, you could create a funnel to make you the ultimate winner, the apex predator.

Since much of this success is real, the concept seems bulletproof and brilliant. But what they don't tell you is that it takes a solid investment of time upfront to create the dream of passive income effortlessly. This is true for all kinds of jobs—if you are successful in them, people start taking an interest in learning how to join, learn what to figure out or do, consume more knowledge, buy more of these courses, and start to spend their own money on different platforms.

The truth about affiliate marketing, and digital marketing in general, is that it's not close to passive income, certainly not at first. Passive income historically ONLY exists in real estate if you can call it passive because you still must research the best investments, know enough not to fall victim to scams or brokers looking to make a buck off you, as well as in the stock market. So, when anyone tells you that it's the equivalent of people who promise a certain return on investment at the stock market, claiming something can give you completely passive income, is usually a fake incentive that's meant to entice you into a deal or into buying their course. Afterward, you're likely to be disappointed and lose some money, time and motivation at the end of that process—or it's just their way of showing off to you while saying that they are not working hard at all while you have to really sweat in order to generate money.

Sure, I can tell you with conviction that if you're successful you can make a lot of money and possibly achieve many dreams, but you don't start with the result you want in the end. A lot of people focus on the result or living the dream but not the work it takes to create it. No one can promise you that if you go into the stock market or open a venture capital firm you're going to live like Warren Buffet or one of the guys on the TV show Shark Tank, but I can assure you that everything starts from hard, long-lasting work. You don't start out at the top of the food chain, you start from a place where you could potentially get eaten, where you're at risk of being someone's prey.

If you expect to do affiliate marketing as a side hustle or just to make a few extra bucks here and there, know that this approach would be a lot more like playing roulette at the casino —you might make money, but it'll be more based on luck than statistics, and there's a big chance you're going to lose that money in the near future if that is your strategy.

The result of the false promises out there is that people dive into the industry, lose money, time, and (the worst of it, I believe) the motivation to move forward and leave their 9-to-5 jobs.

I like to compare how affiliate marketing appears from the outside verses actually entering affiliate marketing to visiting Las Vegas, Nevada. When I first traveled there, I talked to this flight attendant who made a joke about the fact that Vegas flights are always the same—when you fly into Vegas, people are noisy, happy, and you can hear them throughout the flight, but on the return flight it's usually silent because they are exhausted, but also because they likely lost all of their money and left disappointed. This is how the passive income dream and affiliate marketing industry is nowadays...the experience goes something like this:

<u>The Passive Income Dream and Affiliate Marketing Industry:</u>

1. First, someone sees a YouTube video or some Instagram posts for someone making money or spending money or just talking about how easy affiliate/digital marketing or owning a digital marketing agency is, or they hear about someone who lives close to them making money from digital marketing.
2. Then they decide to run some campaigns without having the right assistance or knowledge, they lose anywhere between a couple hundred to a few thousand dollars, and quit the industry frustrated and thinking affiliate marketers are scammers because they bought some useless courses or went to some expensive conferences or masterminds.
3. Since there's no separation between the people who are already inside the digital marketing industry and people that are trying to give it a try, the number of

people trying to get inside is much bigger, since there's bigger rotation, and these people cause a "butterfly effect" when they give digital marketing a shot. They come in with gusto, spend money without understanding the fundamental principles, and cause two major problems. **First**, the amount of money they cumulatively spend is large enough to cause an increase in pricing for everyone. And **second**, they do not understand how policy works and the inner compliance the ad platforms require—they cause these ad platforms to make their algorithms a lot more strict.

4. They churn out, new blood comes in, the cycle continues, and the rotation gets wider. This pattern, by the way, is unlike other industries where people make the shift from being employed by someone to opening their own business. They do not affect any policy or regulation within that industry, and they are far less likely to lose money since they received guidance from the place where they worked or because they worked with a client. Digital marketing is a whole different animal.

If you go into affiliate marketing, or any type of digital marketing—from setting up your own agency to working internally with a specific brand and on to owning your own brand—you have to understand this is a job, a full-time job, just like any other job. It has a lot more flexibility, yes; you can work from anywhere, just like the "digital nomad" dream, but working from anywhere doesn't work for everyone. You have to know yourself well enough to know if that style of work is the right fit for you. Some people lose themselves, some can't concentrate without external parameters, and some just need people around them because that makes work fulfilling for them. In theory traveling to India, Switzerland, or Mexico with your significant other and working from there could sound like a dream. In reality, you need a good Wi-Fi connection, a good desk setup, and strong self-discipline since it's much harder to work when the beach is a two-minute walk from where you live. So, along with being super distracted by all notifications on all the apps you already have on your phone, as well as the distractions of your personal life, you'll find you also need to balance wanting to travel and see the world with the need to actually focus on work.

The fast-paced lifestyles you see on YouTube or Instagram do not match real life. You can't buy a Bentley or your dream house before working hard for those goals. And even when things work well for you, the only thing you can count on is that the next problem is right around the corner. That problem can range from having issues with banks to collecting money from clients, from dealing with policy issues and account bans (from all types, and there are plenty, believe me) to dealing with affiliate networks, advertisers and even partners you're going to have... from designing creatives to editing videos, from making sure tracking works to implementing codes—and, of course, learning new things all the time... That adds up to a ton of dedication, not lounging in the sun for weeks touring around the Mediterranean on your yacht.

A huge thing people overlook is the amount of stress involved. As an agency, you're constantly stressed about keeping your existing clients happy and recruiting more clients. Or, as an affiliate you're trading with your own money, which means that you're likely going to lose at the beginning of the campaign, until you optimize that campaign, as well as losing on bad conversion rates or high-cost days.

Entrepreneurship is hard enough, regardless of what industry and line of work you are in, so just imagine how easy it is to scale up or potentially lose money when we're talking about the internet, and all you need is to add one more 0 at the end of the campaign settings.

. . .

How Your Friends and Family Are Going to Look at You:

To be honest, I don't think most of my family even knows or understands what I do. I don't even think most of the women I've dated could describe my career, no matter how many times I tried to explain, because it's either very technical or it's just too dynamic. Sometimes it's my agency, sometimes I invest in businesses that are unrelated to digital marketing, and sometimes I'm an affiliate for someone else's business...

It's so complex that even within the wide parameters of what I do, I have so many different business models and structures. For instance, one business model would focus on buying media for a product, and another business model would almost make the business relationship seem like I'm their direct partner because I'm so involved.

It's difficult because either I oversimplify it and they don't see the whole picture of what I do, or I go into too much detail and over-explain. Either way, the result is the same—they don't understand the complexities and interrelationships of the various aspects of my work.

The reasons it's super hard to explain, even for younger, more technical people are:

1. People don't believe in easy/fast money, and once you're good you make making money look effortless.
2. People may also be suspicious because it was branded too much like a scam, or it's not a business that people can really measure, such as the success of a restaurant demonstrated by how packed the dining room is and how many tables turn over in a night.
3. Digital marketing and affiliate marketing are fairly new, they only really began to evolve in the last 12 years, and really exploded and expanded in the last six years—and they are the furthest things from conservative businesses.

4. Since they're new, extremely dynamic, and constantly changing, most people in the industry are running/handling campaigns for multiple verticals or niches. It's not like you could explain that you're in a specific industry doing one specific thing, like saying you're a lawyer that specializes in real estate law.

And it's okay that those who surround you don't understand what you do, how to explain it, or really get the ins and outs—the nitty-gritty of what you do—as long as they give you the freedom you need to act and make strategic moves within your business.

Believe it or not, criticism is a major part of working in this industry, especially from older, conservative people. So don't be surprised when you receive pessimistic responses or outright negative accusations.

When I drive my Audi sports car into a gas station, or when I tell people about the expensive neighborhood where I live, what do you think is the first thing that comes to mind? Are you thinking they ask themselves, "How amazing was the school this guy went to?"

Hell no, they think I'm a scammer, that I stole it, or I got it from my family through generational wealth.

Some people are going to think you didn't earn what you have and that you're a type of person who might not believe in hard work or would rather take shortcuts—legal or otherwise. That's because the phenomenal success you can achieve in this field is impressive. Being in the digital marketing industry, we all know that some of these responses or expectations are complete bullshit, and it's as hard a job as anything else that takes time, patience, dedication, and a ton of effort...even though it may look different to the outside world.

You know what makes me question if high schools and universities might be a scam? I've never met a teacher or a professor in college who was actually successfully doing what he taught. The subject was always either something they knew a lot about or something they failed at doing so teaching was their Plan B.

And that's okay, because when you have a lot of knowledge about something, it doesn't mean that you are necessarily good at it, but it means that you could, potentially, be good at teaching it.

The principles I'm about to teach you in the upcoming chapters come from in-depth knowledge *and* personal experience. I hope you'll find them valuable as you advance to apex-level strategy in your digital marketing career.

As you read through these next chapters, keep an open mind and absorb the information that makes sense to you. At the same time, you can use the information in these chapters to identify where you are now, where you want to be, and how you'll go about carving your path through the jungle to get there.

TWO

FULL-STACK VS NON-FULL-STACK MARKETER

Back, in 2010, if you were a media buyer, you would've been able to copy/duplicate whatever was working—the landing pages, pre-landers, offers, and the ad creatives if you were an affiliate—choose one platform that you felt was the easiest for you, then launch a campaign. If you were working for or as an agency, almost any mediocre text you'd written would've worked, so you'd just launch, results would've probably been good, and you would've made some profit.

Since then, results have changed, people have changed, and the industry has changed drastically. Prices are way higher, policy is much stricter, and even offer payouts or the agency model isn't what it used to be.

I remember when HDMI cables were first available, they were so expensive, just like ISPs for internet connections and higher speeds or flatscreen TVs. And just like any new thing, these companies had to adjust in order to survive and stay competitive in the industry. This is exactly what's been going on in the last five years in digital marketing and probably will go on for the next 10 years. Things change quickly. Overnight you could go from being top dog to underdog, and you as a marketer have to adjust.

The only way to adjust is by learning new skills, being less dependent on other people in order to run effectively, and optimizing your campaigns.

This means that you need to be able to:

- Edit videos, at least at the basic level.
- Edit photos, resize and know the basic functions of Photoshop.
- Use Google Tag Manager to add or remove codes.
- Set up events on Google Analytics and understand that platform in general.
- Install and configure apps on Shopify.
- Set up a landing page and make sure you know how to optimize and A/B test it.
- Connect/integrate and deal with API integrations.

Being a full-stack media buyer or digital marketer is a part of a toolset you need in order to reach apex predator status.

These skills, and many more, are what differentiate a mediocre media buyer from a full-stack media buyer, and they would be even more helpful when scaling campaigns. There's a lot less room for flexibility and margin for error when you're spending money faster, when the campaign is at a higher pace, and when you enter the campaign's "scaling mode."

Lucky for you, nowadays we have numerous apps and products that help marketers do just that in a very easy and fast way, but those basic skill sets are something you have to know.

The main reason to know these fundamentals is because if you depend on a graphic designer to edit or create your ads, and depend on a coder to make another landing page for you or implement another code set, things are going to take 5x–10x longer, and that's an unsustainable pace in a world where pausing campaigns isn't good for the account or overall campaign health or for the momentum you have to manage that campaign. You just can't wait for a landing page to be ready in a week when you need to create new variants every couple of days in order to optimize.

A Full-Stack Marketer (FSM) is Two Main Things:

1. Someone who learns these new skill sets, makes sure she knows exactly what she needs to become as self-reliant as possible instead of depending on an external source, person, or team.

2. Someone who goes deep into every media buying platform, instead of focusing solely on Facebook (or whatever social media platform is easy and big right now) as their main ad platform. They risk their own money on testing new campaign structures, they live and breathe the campaigns they manage, and they're always looking to perfect their campaigns, almost to the point of obsession.

Finding these full-stack marketers/apex predators as an advertiser or a brand owner to work for you could be extremely difficult and recruiting them is another challenge. Equally challenging is finding someone who actually wants to run campaigns outside of Facebook and the easier platforms, and finding someone who really cares about the campaign that he works hard for and treats it like his own. So, if you manage to master media buying and digital marketing to the point where you become "full stack," that would almost guarantee you a job at a good company or the ability to easily find people who would want to partner with you. And if you're looking to recruit one, a good option would be taking a good media buyer and just giving her the right tools to grow. That's what a lot of brand, agency, and company owners are doing.

Bottom line, a great full-stack marketer understands how the whole business works and does not just run ads. They know the costs, they know the operational side of things, and they know how to connect with the more technical side—that is, in my opinion, when you really master media buying.

The best kind of a full-stack marketer is someone who doesn't necessarily have to love his job, but he's definitely obsessed with the results he's getting to the point where it becomes about total dedication.

At the end of the day, this industry compared to other industries isn't just that digital marketing is fairly new, it's also undergoing the biggest changes an industry could go through in the short time it's been around. Almost comparable to the Industrial Revolution of marketing in general. And just like anything new, prices are going to stabilize and standards are going to go up. If you're willing to play the game, and you want to play to win, you'll have to unleash the resourceful wolf within. You'll need to learn to be agile and adjust in order to dominate the field.

THREE

"WHERE DO I START?" (AND HOW TO RESTART IF YOU'RE ALREADY IN THE GAME)

For beginners just starting out in this field, I have included small starter guides on how to find yourself within the digital marketing space, and you can always get more on my YouTube channel - @wolfmaor

For intermediate readers and more seasoned professionals, I want to share that I've had times when a part of my business stopped working or didn't make money, and I had to come up with something new. That happens to many people in this industry (and in businesses in general). I'm talking about pivoting and maneuvering in this ever-changing field.

So, if you're already inside the industry, remember that just like great poker players and successful people from the personal development space—even some of the successful business people you've met or known—it's possible to go bankrupt multiple times before these forerunners created stability and true success. You, too, might get into a situation where you need to restart your career and change paths...so use this information to better respond and push forward to help your business and the people around you!

You know the proverb: "Give a man a fish, and you feed him for a day. Teach a man to fish, and you feed him for a life-

13

time." I am trying to teach you how to fish. In these forward-thinking conversations, people ask me, "Okay, what do I do tomorrow? And next week? And next month?" They want to run, make their first buck.

Whatever you read next isn't necessarily going to be extremely practical, but I promise you that after you finish reading, you'll have a simple plan for what you need to do to start gaining traction and understanding what you want to do within this industry. You'll also have the basic knowledge to prepare you for any start, restart, or pivot that happens throughout your digital marketing career. This is where you leap from being weak prey to becoming the strong predator—*you start with the hunter's mindset.*

"Where would you suggest I begin?" is probably the question I get asked and talk about the most, at least twice a week.

This usually comes from people who are in a totally different industry and place in life, such as lawyers or accountants who want to make the shift. Sometimes it'll be folks who are working in the industry, but on a different side, like for example they might be an account manager/affiliate manager (AM) and they want to also try and run some campaigns as affiliates. Or maybe they're working for an advertising agency, and they want to move on to being a brand owner, set up their own agency, or become affiliates.

Well, my first instinct and honest thought is—thank God I don't need to start now. The amount of information, conferences, gurus/teachers/people to follow, and fake gurus to watch out for is crazy. As for the wide-ranging question of "Where should I start?" The only way to really help whoever's asking that is to break it down to the essentials.

Let me start by saying that this is completely dynamic, meaning, if you know for example that you're not the book reader type, or you know that you're an introvert and it's hard for you to talk to people, you have two choices…skip to the next available option and take your chances, or adjust and thrive.

UNLEASH YOUR INNER WOLF

Also, if you know that you have some kind of skill or asset that could be used creatively to get you up and running in the industry, make sure that you fine-tune the ideas in this book to what you have to better serve you, as some of them are more technical and some are personal development related.

Creating and Setting the Right Mindset

Yes, I know, you're keen to get started and/or move up to apex level. And no, I promise, this isn't kumbaya spiritual bullshit. But you *absolutely must have the right mindset* to start your journey from vulnerable prey to rising to the top of the food chain.

When people tell me that they're going to the casino and all they've allowed themselves to lose is $100, I always tell them that's the worst mindset to be in…unless you're really into losing money, which I don't think is why you're reading this book. Even if you look at a casino as offering an entertaining game to pass the time, why not play to win?

Now, don't get me wrong, I'm not suggesting you need to come with an unlimited budget when going to the casino to gamble. And I'm not saying investing a lot in a casino game or any kind of gambling is a wise move, but saying upfront that you allowed yourself to lose puts you in a "loser" state of mind because it's a defensive position to begin with.

Why not say that you're going to stop playing once you win X amount of money because that's a good ratio to what you're investing in playing that casino game for example?

That's a much more positive and empowering mental position to be in.

When Michael Jordan won each championship, he lifted his hand and showed how many championship rings he had already won, and he always had one more finger for the one that would come the year after. That's the mentality that you need to be in when going into this industry.

If you're saying that you're only entering to make $50 more a day, that's the mindset you're going to have when launching a campaign but even worse, that's a prey's mindset—that will allow you to give up instead of learning how to stay the course, or deal with campaigns losing or clients leaving you.

When you're in the hunter's state of mind, you always think of what's next, you look at those goals as milestones, there's never a final "end goal," and there is always another mountain to conquer. Without making sure you're in that state of mind, the odds of you creating a thriving business let alone making money in any business for the long-term will be stacked against you.

Having and Using an Unfair Advantage

People often ignore or disregard their unfair advantages.

Take a minute to consider what I mean when I say that. You likely bring to the table innate gifts, talents, and attributes that correlate with the necessary skills to outpace the competition. For example, you might have a family relative with an advertising agency, or you know someone who's already an affiliate. Another example is that you might live in a city where there's a big hub of affiliate/digital marketers, or you could be using your family's business as your first client and use case, before you try and expand to external clients.

Regardless of where you are now, a great way to start would be mapping out your current assets, skills, and advantages, and —since sometimes we can't see what we have right in front of us because of our unintentional blind spots that we all have —I suggest asking a friend (preferably the one who always tells it like it is) or anyone else that might give you a fresh perspective (like a personal development coach) to sit down with you and map the opportunities you have immediately available.

You'd be amazed how many times people have come up to me and told me they need to make more money and they don't have any ideas. When, in reality, they were manufacturing products for other people and had access to exactly what is working and applicable right now, they simply needed to duplicate that business model and even get the same products at a lower cost, allowing them to be more competitive.

You'd also be amazed at how many times I've seen huge blind spots when people made career choices. For example, someone would tell me he doesn't have time to work on a side project because he wants to be able to spend more time with his kids, and my answer to him was that that's exactly the reason he needs a side project now. Life has a perfect balance. You invest now in something that's going to allow you to spend a lot more time with your kids in the future. You sacrifice one weekend to be able to enjoy four...and those weekends will hold more opportunities because you'll have the freedom to make choices independent of what you once could barely afford.

Understanding that this ability to leverage current assets—people or processes or strategies—is a big blind spot for all of us (including you) is crucial. Even if you're the smartest person ever, you still need someone to point you in the right direction and help you see how sometimes the greatest thing that would move you towards where you want to be the quickest way possible...could be right under your nose.

Below is a list of ideas to brainstorm hidden opportunities to establish your unfair advantage. Use them as inspiration for how to identify them in your life; meaning, don't look for these exact specific things, but use them to open your mind to those opportunities that could be taken advantage of and lead to greater success.

- Having a family (close or distant) business that spends/depends/could use advertising...if they currently rely on a person or agency, can you offer to be the point of contact in front of the agency or internal team they are working with so you could learn?

- Having access (family/friend) to data, which could include many options, from a manufacturing facility that would know what's trending to forums and groups that talk about certain trends. Maybe a friend has access to paid Facebook groups that usually cost money, and he doesn't mind sharing his access or posts from there?
- Living in a small city where you could team up with the marketing expert you knew from high school and learn faster or even work together.
- Knowing someone who did it already, or someone who knows someone who has made it in the industry…could you talk to them and ask them questions? Could you work with them for free?
- Knowing someone who knows a lot of people who spend money online…maybe you could set up an agency together?

Creating and Choosing a Specific List of Sources

Creating a list that would include your "go-to" places where you can learn is important and should be dynamic because that really changes from one person to the next.

The first key is to dedicate time to make a complete list (as extensive as possible) in one sitting—and not just start to scribble a few ideas before you get all excited and dive into the process immediately. The reason for your list has to do with the way you plan and map your advantages and ideas. So that when you fail or get disappointed with one source, you'll come back to your list to consider your next best opportunity. If this list is short, you'll soon come up empty, and then you might not have the motivation to keep going. Instead, if you fill it with plenty of ideas ready for you to explore, when one doesn't work, you'll just move on to the next one.

Why is this list dynamic? Because one person learns through videos, another through reading books. Maybe audiobooks are better for you, or maybe you need to sit in an actual class with people who are leading the pack.

One way or another, what I've found works for a lot of people is dividing the knowledge that's out there into a few segments. Here are some examples:

- "All-in-one" courses.
- "Generic" courses – stuff that would help you get most of the industry but doesn't necessarily have anything to do with digital marketing – like personal development, negotiation courses, books about networking.
- Specific media buying and related courses – it's my belief that whether you're going to be a copywriter or the CEO of the company, you need to learn how media buying works.
- Specific copywriting courses, for example, Facebook public groups, Facebook private groups (paid or invite only), or Affiliate/digital marketing forums (like STM).
- Video libraries with guides (paid or public on YouTube).

When you're researching places to learn from, making sure you have an updated list of categories like the one I provided helps you map all or most of the possibilities you potentially have.

The key to getting in, which I found working for a few people who went through this process with me, is that you first take just one good "all-in-one" course. These are the types of courses that will give you a taste of what digital marketing is like from multiple angles—they have a few talks about copywriting, a few about Facebook and Google, a few about tools like Google

Analytics, and a few about tracking. Those courses are good for several reasons. First, they'll help you really understand *if* you want to get into the industry. Second, they'll help you to begin to understand *where* you want to go within the industry. Do you want to be an affiliate? Set up your own brand? Be a copywriter? Work alone or for a company?

Also, remember—at the end of the day, if you want to be a "full-stack" person, you need to at the very least understand how everything works.

The smartest, most successful people I know in this industry started by owning or working at a call center or copywriting for other people before they opened their own business. When you start "at the bottom" so to speak, learning the essential basics, it's easy to see the mistakes the business is making, how it's operating, and what changes you could make in order to open up a business like this one free of those mistakes, and where you'd optimize it so it'll require less risk and possibly create more value. I always liked the idea of bussing tables at a restaurant I'm going to later buy, start at the place where you'll get the best overall view of how the operation functions and figure out the weak points that the big bosses are probably missing.

Another key would be not spending any money on learning or testing until you use all of the free courses at your disposal, or at least make minimal investment in the really cheap ones. The fact that the content is free or cheap does not mean it's not good. There's so much content out there by Google, on YouTube, and on the internet and social media in general that it's crazy to spend money on a very expensive course that over-promises and most likely will underdeliver.

Moving into Action

At this point with all the research you've done or plan to do, you should start to get a feel for what you want to do inside the digital marketing industry, and you should have a solid, initial roadmap based on what you have in terms of resources and your unfair advantages that you're going to use.

If you feel like you have or need more time (and you probably will) to learn and get a good overall understanding, I suggest going to an event. It could be a smaller event (like a 15-people meetup), a medium size event (up to 150 people), or a large event (up to 10,000 people).

Know that this feeling of being overwhelmed and anxious is normal. It's a cocktail of uncertainty that feels different for every individual. You'll always feel like you have much more to learn, especially if you did not take any action up until now. **Pushing yourself to take action is necessary.** Remember, prey sits and waits to be eaten, hunters *take action.*

Plenty of people get stuck learning the theory, sometimes for years. I don't recommend this approach. Get out there and start moving, even if it's stepping out of your comfort zone to attend a small group or conference where you can start networking which will lead to potential partnerships and tangible steps forward.

Usually, the smaller events are not as overwhelming and you'll get more connections from them, but if you feel like you're a "networking machine" and you have experience with networking, then go ahead and go for the big ones. I always compare the big ones to the Olympics, no athlete really starts there, they spend years training, and I also truly believe that there's more benefit to the intimate events.

The first response I usually get when I dare to make a suggestion like going to an event such as a conference or a mastermind to those who are starting out, or want to move from working for someone else, is that they 1) either don't know anyone, 2) they're afraid (they usually don't say it), or 3) they won't have anything to talk about right away. They worry others might recognize they aren't invested in the industry yet or their nerves kick in. We'll talk about that initial fear later in this book, how natural it is and how to overcome it, but to those people, I say YES! You are correct, everything you fear is real, BUT – it's going to stay that way until you activate your inner wolf and choose to take the fearless route no matter what.

Now, don't get me wrong, going to an event isn't for everyone, and a lot of people make money and thrive without attending any events. But these events could help you accelerate your path, and they work for many if not most in this industry. People gain knowledge, network, and even find their future business partners, friends, and even wife or husband.

I've personally had situations throughout my career where I was stuck, didn't feel like things were moving forward, didn't have any opportunities, and the people I was used to going to events with were not coming to the next one I wanted to attend. For example, I typically went to such events with a team, partners, or just people I knew, but at one point none of them were going to the next event in Las Vegas, and the ones who did go were not people with whom I wanted to interact.

I finally found a friend that had an affiliate and Software as a Service (SaaS) operation in the digital marketing space, so I decided to go with his partner to that upcoming event in Vegas. I reached out to him and asked him how I could help him out, and I agreed to recruit people and hand out flyers at the event for free. That was fine because for me it was a perfect opportunity to not only reach out to new people but also hang around with a team and not feel alone.

Before that trip I was debating whether I was making the right move. It wasn't just about working for free; it was overcoming my ego and a lot of other fears because deep down I was nervous about going. I worried it was the wrong move, and my brain was working nonstop to find logical reasons why I shouldn't go.

I overcame it back then, and what I discovered is that if an event doesn't go as planned, there's always another chance to improve the experience next time. I occasionally still have that old anxiety creep up before a conference, where I ask myself why I even need to attend it and worry my content isn't good enough, or about my ability to maintain focus on clients' campaigns when I'm outside of my normal work routine.

On that specific plane ride to Vegas, I met someone who became a very close friend and my business partner within the next three years.

This story is amazing because it reveals so much:

1. You don't know where the next business opportunity or business partner will come from. You need to reach out and explore chances for opportunities to find you. Nothing happens when you don't make a move, even if it's from home, even when working online. **Make big moves and decisions.** The ball is always in your court. Be the wolf that takes action instead of lurking in the shadows.

2. Your brain is really good at keeping things as they are —it's not aimed towards making you thrive. All it comes up with are ways of making sure you survive by not going through the difficult experiences such as sadness, loss, or negative interactions. **Remember, this is exactly how each new beginning feels,** and we'll talk more about this in the upcoming chapters of this book. I'll also show you how to deal with nerve-wracking challenges. You have to push through the tendency toward stagnation. It's your brain's job to make more excuses and reasons why you shouldn't push boundaries. And it's your powerful inner drive that will overcome the thoughts that try to hold you back.

3. There's always a move to be made. Even when you think you made all the moves, and the next one might feel extreme, but it's still a move. This is true even if you feel like you've lost or made the wrong move. I can't tell you how many times, in hindsight, the bad

decisions turned out to be at the very least neutral ones—sometimes even great ones. Writing this almost feels like writing a religious text for me, since implementing this into my mindset and work routine changed my actions and results so much for the better (in and out of business). But honestly, I can't remember any situation that felt terrible at the time, yet now I can look back at it and say it was either good or sometimes even the best thing that happened to me. Things have a way of working themselves out in the end, they really do.

Now, don't get me wrong...the fact that I had an amazing excursion to the conference in Vegas that ended with me making a friend, business partner and money does not just have to do with my skill set—it has to do a lot with luck. And you increase your luck by getting better at networking, building a name for yourself, and scaling your own brand in a beneficial way. That requires time to accomplish, and not every trip you take is going to be ideal. You really need to suspend all expectations if you have any upcoming trips that offer the chance to network. I could've done all that I did and ended up with none of the above, and I keep reminding myself of that and appreciating the fact that so many positive things did happen.

Here's another interesting example of mindset. I knew a guy who went to school with me. We did our first bachelor's degrees in Israel together. He was never a fast learner or someone you could call smart per se. We finished our degrees, and the guy wasn't working at all even five years after we graduated. When I talked to him, he gave me the feeling that he didn't want to work a junior job or a job that didn't fit him, so he refused to compromise or take a chance on anything else.

Of course, that made me laugh to myself, because that showed the huge gap he has between how he believes things should work and how the world outside actually works. But I also recognized an opportunity—he had a lot of self-confidence, something many people are missing, and he could use that to seek a job and be less disappointed if/when he was rejected because it didn't matter if he was right or not. His perception of reality was what made it real. He was so sure he was worth a lot that he never became disappointed when he wasn't landing job offers because he never felt like he lost a position, he felt that the place lost him. That mindset was rooted more in arrogance than accepting that he might need to take smaller steps to learn more in the long run.

So, I meet people who give me the sense that they think they're too big to start unless they begin as the CEO of Microsoft. I'm exaggerating here, of course, but I'm getting at these basic things:

1. If you can't get a seat at the table, serve water; if you can't get a company to hire you, hand out flyers at an event. Almost no one starts at the top.
2. You learn to be an apex predator. You aren't entitled to be one the second you venture into these wild woods of digital marketing. You may have a lot of potential, but you also need to connect with how the world works.
3. Nothing beats action. Whether you take small or large strides, nothing compares to staying in motion. The best thing to do when you are having a dry season or when you are down is to make some sort of action plan. Acting on that plan will move everything else, even if you think that action doesn't fit you or won't directly advance you, I have a different viewpoint: it will in the end.

Knowing How to Ask

Throughout your career, you're going to meet people who could have valuable information for you, on online forums or group chats, at conferences, in person or virtually.

Make sure you learn how to ask questions successfully and show active listening skills when industry professionals are answering your questions. Either be prepared with a list of specific things you're wondering about or just come up with a template for how to ask questions.

Even before you ask questions or engage, understand that:

1. This person is not working for you, he does not owe you anything.
2. He has likely talked with 10 people already today and is going to talk to tens or hundreds more. He doesn't have all day to chat, so your questions need to be narrowed down and specific.
3. Remember, this person does not know your product, has not seen your website, and does not have time to go into your account and audit it. You need to explain everything quickly.

A good idea, for example, is:

"How do I do X? I've tried A, B, and C, and every time I do it creates ____. Do you have any experience with that?"

A bad generic, wide-ranged question would be:

"How do I scale on Facebook?" or "How do I decrease prices on Google?" That leaves the person in front of you with no good way of answering.

A question needs to be specific, and it also needs to be:

- Realistic in terms of how long the answer is going to be, you can't ask someone "how to attract women to me?" but you can ask "what kind of shoes are now trending if I want to pick up women at a shoe conference?" a weird example but you get what I mean.

- Specific in terms of how narrow it is, you need to specify what you do, what you tried and what results are you looking for or what problem you encounter every time you try.
- Informative, remember that this person does not know anything about your business or maybe even industry, you must be clear and supply them with that information, but not too much information, for example - wide things like the average AOV (Average Order Value) in the industry or specific things like what you've tried in the past.

We're going to talk more about how to directly communicate via text and email while respecting someone's time later in the book. There's a chapter dedicated to this.

Circling back, a good example of a template or of questions that could be answered within a 10-minute conversation would be:

"I've tried running these types of ads on Facebook, and every time I do it, I get banned. Do you know of any problem with this specific ad that you see?"

—Or—

"My campaigns are doing great on Facebook. My structure is XXX and every time I try to get the budget up over YYY my CPA (Cost Per Action) goes crazy. What would you do?"

I can't list the broad range of questions people asked me— ones I really wanted to help them with—but ones where the question was too broad—I had to ask them to give me more information about the account or campaign. As a consultant you want to help people, sometimes even for free, but in order to really give an informative, actionable response, sometimes you have to be able to visualize that specific scenario.

Without following these rules, you won't be able to extract

everything you can and implement it into your business or campaigns. Even if the person you're talking to is an expert in a specific field, you want to make sure you ask them something that they can answer and you can implement at the end of the day. So, make sure you prepare questions that have to do with what you want to learn from that conference as a way of being proactive before any conference.

Beginnings Are the Worst...But They Do Get Better!

If you're starting out or planning a change, these next few lines are going to be a game changer for you, they made a big change for me.

In the first book of the Bible, the Book of Genesis, the first five verses say something that many believe is God's way of dictating how life works and how you should live life.

It goes like this: "In the beginning, God created the heavens and the earth. **Now the earth was formless and empty, darkness was over the surface of the deep**, and the Spirit of God was hovering over the waters."

Now I'm not trying to make you religious or anything, I'm not a religious person myself, but I do find that verse extremely interesting. What I want you to take from it is that every beginning is formless and empty. It's always dark, and there will be times when you feel the walls are closing in on you. That's how it's supposed to feel, and if you've done it enough times (begun or started over in business) you know it always feels the same. The new beginnings you've faced might not have the same level of darkness and emptiness, but they all feel similar.

There is no worthwhile growth without that feeling, and it's an unavoidable part of life for everyone.

Comfort = Stability = Certainty = No Growth
Darkness/Emptiness = Unstable = Uncertainty = Growth

Before pushing ourselves into a new space, everything we already know is comfortable to us, hence our "comfort zone."

Even if that place is complete shit, it's still shit that we already know, so it's comfortable.

Every *genesis*, every new beginning, is the point where you **move from certainty to uncertainty.** In order to grow you have to expand out of and away from your comfort zone, and slowly you increase your range of comfort. It takes practice, but eventually you broaden your horizons and find yourself at home in a space that used to seem frightening because it was unfamiliar. Now it's great—and way better than before you took the leap! Keep that in mind each time life asks you to move beyond your current experiences into foreign territory. The universe is always working for you if you allow it to and trust yourself and the process.

Since we're already into that passage from the Bible, the last thing I would like to share is a conversation I enjoyed when talking to a rabbi about the final part of that sentence: "and the Spirit of God was hovering over the waters." During the beginning stages of newness and change, sometimes hovering is necessary, waiting with a positive expectation of what might unfold in the future that you can't yet see. Allowing yourself to be still and let inspiration come to you can be challenging.

In business and life, many people are pushing their expectations onto a situation. For example:

- Starting to think that you can't do it, can't take the next step.
- Second-guessing yourself or assuming you know what another person is doing or thinking.
- Saying to yourself or other people that things aren't working out for you.
- Looking for external justifications why things aren't working out. For example, just because the business next to yours closed (as research shows many businesses fail within the first year) you assume that will be your fate as well.

All of these negative thought patterns are pushing you into the exact situation you fear, when instead you should be hovering, looking for an opportunity that meets your preparation. In order to move confidently and push towards your goals (not just business but any goals in life) you need to make the decision that you are done with explaining or accepting the current situation. You are done looking for external justifications. You will no longer dive into negative thoughts when you describe your situation to yourself or other people.

By choosing at times to hover at the beginning of an endeavor, you can analyze the actions you've made. You still should be goal oriented as fuck, but you move into understanding that success now equals making the moves that, in your strategy, will bring you to your goal in a thoughtful, more confident way. The truth is you are only in charge of the decisions you make, not the results you receive.

MOVES => MEASURED BY => ~~RESULTS~~ THE FACT YOU MADE THE MOVE

When we focus solely on the *results* we received and not the *actions* we're taking towards making our goals happen, we're going to end up frustrated very quickly. So often even if you make the perfect decisions and play the perfect game, you're still going to get into a situation where you lose, because you just can't control all the variants. We must resist falling into the trap of searching for *justifications* like research or statistics or look to other people or others' excuses for why failure happens. We'll find research shows how many people are losing money when they open up a new business, how many affiliates lose their seed money or how much the digital marketing/agency/affiliate game isn't what it was used to be.

In truth, for every research quest you embark on, for every Facebook post that talks about going in one direction, there will be ten others saying the complete opposite. For every article saying that coffee is good for you, there's another that says that it's bad. Again, focus on the actions you're taking, and do not judge the results as a failure or a challenge to the success awaiting you. They're all lessons along the way.

Accelerating Your Journey

While you decide what route you're going to take in this industry, what suits you, and you keep on gaining more information and knowledge, there are a few important actions you could consider taking to accelerate your journey. One would be going to work for 6–12 months at an agency or a brand on their digital marketing team, even if that job isn't the best one you could find in terms of hours or a paycheck.

That could be the best education you're going to have in this industry, because they would teach you how things actually work and give you practical advice, at least from their perspective. You would also get to spend other people's money and not risk your own.

Some potential pitfalls that could arise from this option are:

1. You'll get used to working for someone else and this might create for you a "golden cage" situation where it's harder for you to step out into entrepreneurship. If it's a good workplace, they're going to keep giving you more responsibilities, more benefits, and more money to encourage you to stay. If the conditions are mediocre or even bad, then it wouldn't hold you back and even encourage you to leave with your newfound knowledge, but that's a rare case. Just be sure to keep your ultimate goal in mind when working for someone else.

2. Some businesses work in a different ways than others, and that might offer a negative way of looking at things. For example, you would think that getting prepaid for campaigns, charging a specific amount or %, is usual. However, this is just the way that specific

business chose to structure their pricing—and it doesn't mean that it's the perfect or ideal model you need to follow or the only correct pricing method to use.

3. I would look at what mistakes are being made or what could be done differently in order to create a better business in any way and write it down so I could implement it into my brand or agency later on, do this WHILE working for that other business, you do not want to forget things later, it's easier to delete some notes than to remember what you wanted to write.

4. I've seen some businesses create and use scarcity to keep employees on the job, meaning, they would create the illusion that what they are doing could only be done with the company's resources and you are worth nothing on the outside. Be wary of this approach and lack mindset. It's either controlling/manipulative or a very negative way of perceiving the full breadth of financial opportunities in this industry.

The truth is that even if they do have some IP (intellectual property) or a patent, there's always something else that can be done in the same space or even using the same approach but in a cheaper way. None of us needs to reinvent the wheel, but we can increase the diameter and add more spokes. At the end of the day, even their business was not built in a day, and yours will benefit from your broader mindset when you open it.

Another potential action you could take to accelerate your journey could be one-on-one talks and even paid consultations with people you know are making or getting the results you want to achieve for yourself. Out of all the paid promotions out there, finding a coach or consultant would be my #1 recommendation in terms of where to spend your money. After that my #2 recommendation would be to attend masterminds and smaller conferences.

This could be a very good example of how to learn and move your digital marketing career faster, as long as you understand that this is just a milestone, another station on the way to your goal of really getting into being your own boss and living a life of freedom where there's no cap on how much you could make.

Some ideas possible solutions to these problems could be:

1. Setting up a specific length of time to work there, for example, one year where you tell yourself that almost no matter what happens you're going to continue your entrepreneurship journey and that you've dedicated that specific time for learning and not to stay. *This is so important because it creates a goal-oriented mindset, a starting and finishing point for that specific segment in your life, and it will help you be more aware and focused on what you want to get out of that situation.*

2. Knowing that these workplaces are going to create reasons for you to stay—they'll range from good ones, like better salary and benefits, to bad ones, like making you feel like you can never do it by yourself or creating a false sense of dependence. Be wary of those tactics. Some places use that psychology—they'll make you think they either invested huge sums of cash into the business (so you can never hope to start with more modest means) or they'll make you think that the technology they patented is the only way to have success. They might even have non-compete contracts in place with certain connections or competitors stating you can't work in this field when you finish working with them. You may have to abide by these for a period of time, so be aware this is a tactic and guard yourself against unfair clauses in your

employment contract. Keeping in mind ahead of time what you want for your future is KEY.

I know this may seem like a lot, but it's important for me to share as much information as possible so it not only applies to those inside the digital marketing industry, but also for people considering the next step in their career.

Everything starts and ends with mindset. So many of us live inside a place that limits us and prevents us from moving on to something new…and often we don't even realize it, even though others can often see what we can't see in ourselves.

Understanding more about *yourself,* the advantages and disadvantages you have, is the step that comes before understanding what your goals are. These two are essential in order to move to the next step—creating that list of tasks you're going to take action on (move into action). Being organized is a big part of knowing where you are in this dynamic and complex process. Unfortunately, too many people start with action instead of the first crucial intellectual parts needed before taking action.

Finally, it's important to understand this flow. It ends just like it begins—with the mind and a plan for how to overcome internal difficulties. It's easy to think and say certain things when you're alone or even when you're with someone you trust. It's a whole different feeling when you are out in the field. If you take this chapter and adopt it, repeat it, and learn it, this information will become valuable in any job or project you attempt, and these suggestions will create a much easier path to guide your way. It certainly has for me.

The following chapters discuss how to remain excited while still protecting yourself in your new element by limiting the number of people who could potentially mislead or even scam you. I hope it will reduce some of your naïveté as your venture into this industry while still maintaining your enthusiasm.

FOUR

"FAKE GURUS"

While searching for and finding places where you'll be able to learn, you're going to encounter what people call "fake gurus." There's just no way to avoid them. The fact that they are getting a whole chapter in this book should tell you what a big problem this is. It goes beyond trying to teach something that you don't know that much about or trying to look better, it's an entire fakeness mentality that's out there, and it's growing by the day.

I used to think that "those who can't do, teach" was based on simple logic and on the common question that "If that person knows it so well, why doesn't he just do it? Why would he spend his time teaching others?" or "If that person actually knew how to make money, he would've just generated it," or "No one teaches how to generate money for real." I totally understand why people think that way.

As I continued going through my coaching sessions, I learned that people who understand stuff in theory at a high level could become good teachers. It doesn't necessarily mean that they are actually able to do it on their own, or, another case is that these people do have their own business, generating money, and they really feel like there's "enough for all of us to eat," and they don't mind sharing, or they even feel compelled to share their knowledge and experience (like me).

Coming from Israel, with the Israeli direct approach and mentality, I personally like it when people put their cards on the table. I hate the small talk people have at the start of a meeting, and I despise when people lie or are being inauthentic, but that's also a part of the culture I come from, and I get that not all people are the same.

To simplify, a "fake guru" is someone who would:

1. Overpromise and underdeliver.
2. Use fake results, made-up testimonials, or fabricated case studies to sell a brand or a service/product. Sometimes that product doesn't even exist, or if it does it's very low level, like a bad course that teaches nothing/has negative reviews or bases its recommendations on unachievable results for new businesses.

By that definition, by the way, anyone who also has a SaaS product (for example) that doesn't really do much would be a fake guru, it doesn't just have to be a course or a digital product.

For example, there are many campaign manager products out there that claim to have better results than when running on the regular Facebook ads manager, and they claim to have an "AI smart system." When in reality, they know that their system isn't AI based, it's not really doing anything else besides changing the Facebook ad manager user interface (UI) into some other UI that might be more "comfortable" to look at. In the end, it doesn't do what they promised, like get better results on clients' campaigns.

Last time I was at an event in Ibiza I talked to a woman who, once she heard that I'm a speaker that goes on stages and talks at events, immediately said, "Oh, you're one of those gurus?" in a way that sounded like she didn't respect them in the least.

So, I think it's important to separate and kind of "normalize" the discussion about who's a fake guru and who isn't.

The fact that someone goes on stages and gives talks and/or creates a YouTube account and uploads videos to promote his interest does not make him a "fake guru." **We all get up in the morning to pursue our own interests** and that's okay, even when that person doesn't have the knowledge you were looking for or his level isn't on par with what you'd expect.

This scenario turns problematic when someone pushes it over that limit and attempts to sell something that isn't real, over-promises and under-delivers, uses bogus case studies, and purely, obviously lies. Usually, these people know full well they're fakes—this is deliberate scamming.

How to Recognize & Avoid Fake Gurus

1. For starters, remember that you don't need to buy any course or follow any specific person. There's a lot of knowledge out there for free. Start by going that route. It's a foolproof way to avoid scams.

2. Be wary if a person invests too much in the image they present—meaning they share too many pictures that flaunt their wealth or possessions. If they boast about how they achieved their success and their life on social media circles around this showiness, that would be a big red flag. *Genuine people and real teachers don't need to prove what they have or how they got it. Leonardo DiCaprio doesn't walk around posting pictures of his abs or spending heaps of cash. If someone wants to work with him, great. If not, there's always someone else. Most of the good, or even amazing, teachers and knowledgeable people I know help for free, answer people on Facebook, and don't have a huge social media following.*

3. A fake guru's main product is themselves. They are making more money showcasing a product or strategy than from actually working as what they say they are

—agency, brand, or SaaS product owner. How can you spot them? They put themselves at the forefront on social media, at conferences, and whenever they're talking to people. It's all about them. *This is a bit tricky as you can't go check their accounting to know what they're making money from, but you'll see this type of person and learn to easily recognize them over time. Some of them are pushing their persona so much that I'm amazed others are still falling for it. Every post on Instagram is like: "I do consultations, dm me."*

4. Research reviews about them, these usually do not lie. Try and get reviews from people who actually bought their course, book, or videos and do not buy till you do your due diligence. Also consider that people are not always going to tell you the truth when posting a public post, so you really need to DM or ask people who trust you and that know you already in order to really get the truth, most of the time you'll even get suggestions for free advice or just a better person to learn from.

5. Low quality content—you'll see them posting content just for posting content, even when it's just "Instagram style" inspirational quotes that sound like stuff you'll find in a Chinese fortune cookie. I've seen people post stuff on twitter every couple of hours "business quotes" that are so simple or stupid it was obvious that they have a virtual assistant do that for them.

6. If you do decide to learn from somewhere or someone that asks you to pay for it - usually the best method would be paying for a one-on-one with someone you respect or whose content you like.

"Big Names"

I'd say 30% of the people for whom I've consulted for at least an hour name-drop who they think of as big names inside the industry, alongside with the exits they've done.

Most of them felt at the beginning that these people were an inspiration, and they were copying whatever worked for successful people. They believed that because they were mirroring what the big names were doing, they were on their way to success themselves.

In reality, some (even many) of these big names are part of churning out marketing schemes and quick fixes versus sustainable strategies. Here is often what has happened in these cases:

1. They have been misled—the exits they think happened - never happened, it was all a part of a PR company campaign to capitalize on new interest from more naïve people in the industry. Or if the exit did happen for $XX million, it was spread out over a number of years. Chances are, only a small portion of it was cash, and there were likely a lot of other contingencies to it. Basically, when you look behind the scenes, you'll find it wasn't as impressive as it seemed.

2. The name-droppers try to work with those big names or get into business with them…and end up working for several months with zero movement. At best, the idealist realizes the big name's results aren't what he thought. At worst, the idealist is going to be taken advantage of and thrown away like yesterday's garbage, all their effort for nothing. No one deserves that.

3. The idealist tries to work on her own project and ends up growing complacent and unmotivated very quickly, because she's comparing herself to the big names. However, she doesn't know the full reality of

the big name's scenario and how hard it truly was for that famous person in the beginning. And she'll never know how big that guru's unfair advantage was or what economic advantages that famous person started with back when they began. Things have changed so much in 10 years, we're not comparing apples to apples nowadays, because what worked then may not work at all now, and to base success on someone else's unknown advantages and starting point years ago is not guarantee of current or future success.

Looking at big names is similar to looking at beautiful guys or girls on Instagram or TikTok who are trying to sell you on a weight loss diet or skincare product to make you look like them. Even if in that venue you don't give them actual money, it's still at best an unfair comparison and at worst a hoax—either way, it should be taken with a grain of salt. Yesterday's apex predator could be tomorrow's prey if they haven't taken time to pivot and grow with new strategies for changing times.

Industry Changes and Adjustments You Need to Make

The world is dynamic. Through my agency clients, my businesses, and even some of the affiliate offers I've run, I've gotten to learn more about different industries, niches, and regulations. My conclusion is that the digital marketing industry is probably the most dynamic and frequently changing industry I've seen. Not only that, but it also always seems like if even one small parameter changes, then the whole equation can change.

This is not only because the industry is new, but also because it's not just dependent on the platforms and companies that are changing. Outcomes can depend on the specific sub-industry/brand/client that you're running and all the regulations that are impacted by any changes, new regulations, the stock market, and the constant bidding auction everyone is taking a part of.

It could be that one day there are policy or compliance changes on the ad platform's side or the offer/client's side, or it could be that the algorithm changes, and what used to work for you no longer does. Sometimes it even shifts within the whole industry—within days.

As the agency model changes, the affiliate game changes, and even how easy it used to be selling on Amazon changes. That's a big reason why I'm not writing about trends or "waves" you can catch. I want to give you the tools to act on any change the industry forces on you and your business.

One easy way I use to recognize changes is when people from outside the industry tell me about something that they are going to try, a "new opportunity," something that I have already heard about at least twice that week. For example, when I went to get my BA degree, so many people who had nothing to do with marketing started talking to me about this new thing "drop shipping" that everyone is doing. I already knew that this opportunity was well past its prime, anticipating that policy and compliance would tighten up around that strategy soon. And so it did—PayPal made it extremely hard to sell as a drop shipper, Amazon killed a lot of the stores, and even Shopify went on to receive customer service complaints and close down shops.

So you have these continuous layers of adjustments you need to make:

- Algorithm changes on the ad platform.
- Regulatory changes on the ad platform and on the product/industry level.
- Offer and trend changes—what's trending up and down. For example, A/C when it's hot in certain geographies and loans increase when a recession hits.
- Pricing goes up and down throughout the year and maxes out in some industries by the end of the year, each year.

- Conversion rate changes between times of year and demand for certain products.
- Different bidding and campaign structure types - this could be learned by either watching FB groups and X (formerly Twitter). People post new ideas there, as well as sharing them at conferences and masterminds, but regardless, this should also be tested throughout your campaign's life.
- New products that could help you track, optimize, or create better creatives.
- New creative and prelander/advertorial angles for different campaigns - as people see more and more of the same ads they would need something fresh.

Knowing these changes happen all the time will help you in 2 key areas:

1. Adjusting accordingly—for instance, Q1 should be best to test and run Ecom products and Q4 should be best for loans and search/content arbitrage campaigns.
2. Making sure you're not committed or "married" to strategies that work currently, so you'll have the ability to recognize these changes, the predictable changes and the non-predictable ones and make the shift fast.

When people can't adapt, they start losing money.

This industry requires constant maintenance, if you want to grow or even just keep the clients / campaigns that you're currently running, there's just no way around it, every business that doesn't learn and adjust withers, there is no staying in place or surviving, you either grow and learn, or you die.

To summarize, here's a list on what you should be aware of:

- When people outside of the industry already know about it, the market is probably already flooded and you need to come up with something extremely creative or just move on to the next thing.
- If you plan to copy a certain model, at least have some kind of an unfair advantage, like for example, the ability to get big clients through a big partnership if you're running an agency or a celebrity endorsement if you're opening a brand.

When you don't work for someone, regardless of how much time you've been on your own, you'll always have the fear of instability. It could be a client that you're afraid will leave you soon, a campaign that's running well that you're afraid will stop, or it could be PTSD from having accounts banned on Facebook. You're going to experience a minor level of daily fear, and that doesn't get much better with time, from my experience, but you *will* get better at managing it.

Whether it's the fear of your employer letting you go or the entrepreneur's fear I just mentioned, there is no way of evading fear or the "hard" part. Don't blame yourself if you feel it, because sometimes in life you just have to choose between fears and pain, at least the pain and fear of entrepreneurship is a lot more rewarding.

Things change all the time, that's probably the only thing we know for certain. Your campaigns are going to stop working for some reason and most of your clients are going to stop working with you at some point.

You have two options.

One is to let that fear take control of you and act as though you're experiencing the end of times every day. When that client sounds like they are going to leave you, you'll be terrified. When that campaign has a bad day, you're going to have a bad day.

—OR—

You could understand that you're riding a wave right now,

and every wave ends some time—it could be tomorrow, it could be next week, and it could be in a year. Make sure you ride it the best you can, extracting everything possible from it…and then go out and find the next wave.

THERE'S ALWAYS ANOTHER WAVE.

Someone is making money from something, and if you're smart enough to read this book and invest in yourself, you are smart enough to learn something new.

It might sound like a cliche, but life is too short to go through it suffering.

Personal Development Is Key

I once told someone from outside of the industry that I go to therapy, and even went to couples therapy, and he asked me, "How bad can your relationship be that you had to go to therapy so soon?" That made me laugh because, for me, it's like someone would've told me that he has someone cleaning his house daily or weekly, and you would've asked him, "How dirty is your house that you have to clean it daily?"

One of the biggest things I noticed when I walked around my first conference, and when I started talking to people and the idea of personal development came up, was the number of people who either are in some sort of therapy, go to coaching, or are doing and have done personal development seminars. Compared to the rest of society, the ratio is huge—personal development and therapy is key in this industry.

Since kindergarten, I told my mother that the paintings I painted were all in black and that might mean that I'm sad and that was the first time I experienced therapy. This was not a frowned upon notion in my family, they were supportive of it. Since then, I went on to 37 more therapists throughout my life because I changed locations and because in my early years, I did not have money to go to private therapy sessions.

So, I fully understand the amount of resilience one needs to develop, and the inner skills required in order to get around in this big wide world.

If someone says they are just able to cope with the rollercoaster of making huge sums of money one day, starting to dream about the life you're building for yourself, and the next day the campaigns just stop because of an error or a client leaves you or the account gets banned—without any type of drugs/coaching or therapy—they are fooling themselves or are not pushing themselves to the limits mentally and emotionally.

Going to therapy or couples therapy has nothing to do with how good or bad you feel or how good or bad the relationship is...my view is that entrepreneurship is hard, in any field, and when you manage lots of business relationships, when you have to be stressed out about platforms, advertisers, clients, banks, cashflow, managing partnerships and so much more, the best way to really push yourself forward is having a big support team behind you. Always. Especially when you have to adapt and adjust to so many changes, or you've rebuilt your whole business from scratch (possibly over and over). Without a healthy outlet, you'll likely explode, crash, and burn like many others I've seen throughout my time in this industry.

No one can coach themselves. We all have blind spots, so everyone needs to have at least one mentor, one person they can consult with, who either has done it or just really cares about you. This person must have no agenda other than helping you become more successful, and if that person is a professional, what more can you ask for?

I want to share two important, if not life-changing, things I've taken from my therapy and coaching sessions:

One of the biggest is that we all carry things from our past that, to some degree, impact how much we believe we deserve something good. It could be feeling worthy in our relationships, it could be with our family, it could be our relationship with and attitude toward money, or maybe how we look and react to our business partners. At the end of the day, **everyone has a limit on**

how much they believe they deserve something good. It took me a while to really understand how deep this goes.

Negative Mental Cycle

Here I'm going to simplify the idea as much as possible. The negative mental cycle goes something like this:

1. Someone, deep down, doesn't believe _____. Let's say they don't believe they deserve to make a lot of money. Deep down they think they're somehow unworthy. Maybe they grew up in poverty, or even if they were "comfortable" growing up, maybe others around them had negative views of money; maybe Dad warned "money's the root of all evil," or Mom affirmed "money doesn't grow on trees," or Grandma said, "you have to work so hard to have money, and there's never enough," or Grandpa berated the person as a child, "You don't have what it takes to make it in the business world and be wealthy." You get the idea—these negative thought patterns are subversive. Negative messages become ingrained until we don't even realize they're part of our mindset. They can be deeply damaging at a fundamental level.

2. This person trying to make good money going into business in digital marketing would end up looking for proof of why these negative thought systems are right—statistics, academic studies, other people who think like them, articles. It doesn't matter that there are even more people, articles and studies that show the complete opposite.

3. When a certain situation appears, they are going to interpret it as the reason why things aren't working for them, even though to others who are looking from the

sidelines the two don't have anything to do with each other.

4. They are going to sabotage their own efforts, relationships, and business, acting on what they believe deep within...because it proves to themselves that their small story is right—they don't deserve that wealth, or better yet, they and their negative conditioning were right all along: life's too hard, you never catch a break, money doesn't fall in your lap, a great relationship isn't meant for me, no one understands my situation and what I'm going through, why did I bother when I knew what would happen right from the start. When these negative thoughts draw to them proof of their accuracy, it becomes a self-fulfilling prophecy.

5. They revert back to #1, because that reinforces their initial beliefs.

Let's use a more specific example.

I have a good childhood friend who's very good-looking and works as an international model. He dates only extremely beautiful women. He wants and has always wanted a serious relationship, but every time he gets into a relationship, he begins to believe the woman is being unfaithful to him. It doesn't matter how many times this plays out, it's the same story. No matter how much they insisted they were faithful, he would still believe they cheated on him.

He would see his girlfriend in bed, looking at her phone and he would immediately put her to the test...if he gets close to the phone and she shuts off the phone, she must have something to hide (his interpretation). If she just happened to close an app at the time of his approach, he saw that as proof. He took that as if she wasn't currently cheating, then she was about to do it.

The fact that this kept happening, exactly the same way, over and over with many women—and even having solid, committed relationships didn't make him stop and see if *he might be doing something wrong*. That it had nothing to do with his partners, its highly doubtful all of them were cheaters. Obviously, this is a huge blind spot for him, and his negative expectations led him down the same lonely road. If someone really believes a true, good, stable, loving relationship is something that could happen to him, he is going to see things differently than my friend did. What if one of those women had closed her phone because she was preparing a nice surprise gift for him? Or maybe she closed her phone because his presence was more important to her, and she wanted to give him her full attention?

Someone who really believes that he deserves that good relationship would not have acted in the same suspicious way all the time, every time. He sabotaged himself by sticking to his inherent negative beliefs, even when these negative expectations left him continuously disappointed.

Better to be right than happy…? I don't think so.

And this same mindset challenge goes for people who are in a business relationship. For instance, say someone watched his dad lose all of their savings, or maybe his uncle kept telling stories about how he got screwed by a business partner. That kid went through life looking at situations through the lens of that exact story. Now he's an adult with those same limiting beliefs. If you become his business partner, he's going to think you lose, steal, or cheat regardless of how trustworthy you are.

<u>How to Recognize People Who Do Not Believe They Deserve Wealth</u>

First, as I said, every one of us (to a certain extent) has an area in our lives where we don't really believe we deserve everything we want. It will serve you well to learn to recognize people who have negativity in general or have negativity specific to business.

Second, the only way to recognize someone like that is, unfortunately, often by waiting for a specific situation that will trigger their negative belief system. Fortunately, the people who have the most damaging belief systems are more easily triggered.

This is one example of how this could look:

1. The person becomes unreasonable when triggered. Their reaction is way beyond the norm and is beyond the current situation. In other words, they escalate very quickly; they go from 0 to 60 in seconds. Their brain interprets the situation as unreasonable beyond the ability of logic to intervene.
2. They disregard any simple logic the situation contains or that you might present to them. Fear and survivalism replace all logic. Their brain is only focused on saving them / getting them out of the current situation.
3. You will not be able to talk any sense into them while this is happening. This likely has to do something with their past you cannot control.

How to Fix the Situation or Act When This Occurs

1. Here's the good news and bad news altogether—you can't control others' triggers or have any impact on them. These people are going full speed on a set of train tracks that were laid into the groundwork of their minds years ago. It has nothing to do with you or what you did, so don't feel bad or second-guess yourself when faced with such a visceral reaction.
2. Even if you can control it a bit, you're just delaying the inevitable. You've just earned another tour on the train ride, as the next episode or triggering event is likely just around the corner. This is because their brain is trained to think in a certain way, and it's going to look

for the next possible place to find familiarity in the cycle again.

3. You need to ask yourself if this situation is tolerable to you. If you decide that in order to keep making money with this person and keep the business going, you are willing to go through this each day and in every similar situation, **do not delude yourself that this is ever going to change or be solved**. If you do choose to stay, knowing it won't change, then remain in the situation because you truly believe that you deserve wealth, and this is just your way of achieving it.

FIVE

DEALING WITH "THE CYCLE"

N ow you can see how just about everyone, including you, has a story inside their head telling them they don't deserve something. It could be a perfect partner, or money, or some other inadequacy.

It doesn't matter who you are or what you started with in life or how far you've come, there's always a belief and a story to back it up, one that helps us see that we are right every time something happens. We continue to train our brain by campaigning to everyone we know about this belief. Even when things do not work out in a way that correlates with our belief, we mentally arrange our memories and understanding of events so that they fit.

I want to share with you a personal thought about what we tell ourselves and how things work out in our minds. This is something I came up with when I went through two weeks of a deep depression. When it ended my therapist asked me what made it disappear, and I didn't really know how to respond, so I decided to do some digging. I went way down the rabbit hole on this one—and I found out two major things that became like rules in my life and had a HUGE impact on how I see things:

. . .

Life Rules

Rule 1:

When someone asks you what's wrong with you/your life/why you are depressed or sad, what usually comes out is a story, sometimes the story will have multiple angles or layers.

- "The relationship I have with my parents isn't the way I want it to be,"
- "I don't talk to my sister,"
- "Things aren't working out with my job,"
- "Clients are leaving me,"
- I'm single and can't get into a relationship."

What I found out is that **1+1+1+1+1 in those situations isn't worth 5, it's worth 20** *because when we add those things together in one conversion the sum of them is way heavier than each one separately.* **The conclusion:** make sure you do not repeat the same negative story to yourself and other people because it only trains your brain into thinking about it more and creates a fixation. If you're adding multiple stressors, it becomes a lot heavier and more dramatic to deal with, this is nothing less than poison.

Rule 2:

- I came up with the following mental response that connected everything I learned from going down that rabbit hole: When I **rationalize** a situation, I **legitimize** that situation, I get **fixated** on that situation, and I lose **motivation** to fix or move on from that situation.
- At first that might not sound straightforward, but I promise you, this is a sentence that, when you understand it, could change your life, let's repeat it just one more time before I explain and dig deeper:
- When I **rationalize** a situation, I **legitimize** that situation, I get **fixated** on that situation, and I lose **motivation** to fix or move on from that situation.

. . .

<u>Breaking Down Rule 2:</u>

To really understand the key to this sentence, what you first need to know is that our brain has two functions:

- Add information
- Duplicate information

Our brains <u>cannot remove</u> information, and the memory is <u>unlimited</u>.

When we tell our brain a story, the brain asks itself: does this guy really believe this story? And it could be the biggest lie ever, but if we really believe it and tell our brain that story *over and over* its going to act just as if this <u>story is real</u> and create a barrier between us and life that would act as a protective shield from that situation happening to us. By the way, that is why when people want to buy a new car, they start seeing more of that vehicle on the road—it's the same mechanism.

<u>So when we are depressed, or sad, and try to think of why:</u>

1. We start by telling ourselves and the outside world a story, even if this story is not true, or just a part of how we interpret the situation, we explain or justify what's wrong with us, and we **rationalize** the situation.
2. When we do that, we essentially breathe life into a situation and approve it. We make it seem as if it really happened, as if our interpretation of it is real. As soon as it's accepted, we **legitimize** it.
3. As soon as the situation is legitimized, we create a **fixation** on it, because we tell it to many people, thereby training our brain like you train a muscle when working out, so it knows the story quickly and

can recall it in detail. Then we create a comfort zone by doing that—even if it's the shittiest place you have ever been (in your mind or in reality), it's still a comfort zone because it's familiar. Sometimes even the shittier the better because that protects us and gives us a reason for why we're not trying to push ourselves further.

4. When the comfort zone is set, it's secure and we don't want to move out of that into insecurity, so we lose the **motivation** that we would've had if only we would've lost that story and kept pushing ourselves. We lose motivation because:

- We now have a solid reason for why things aren't working for us.
- Ego problems, we've now gone on a campaign and told everyone that this is the reason we can't move, we lost, etc.
- It's easier to repeat this story than trying to push ourselves again into the unknown.

You know how it is when something happens to you, good or bad, and you tell everyone? You call anyone who'll listen and explain. You post it in your Instagram stories and make sure everyone knows. Every time you do this, you train your brain to think that exact way! You **rationalize, legitimize, fixate** and lose **motivation** at the end of it.

How This Impacts Your Reality

Someone opened a business, that business had two other partners, three in total, that business shows signs of failing, and that someone ended up not having more cash to put into the business or…deep down they stopped believing in the business to put cash into it. One day his partners decide to cut that business, stop the bleed, and move on.

That person goes to his family, his girlfriend, his other partners, and his friends and tells them they've worked super hard, lost money and time, prioritized that business, and those partners decided to up and leave the business one day.

That's his interpretation of that situation; he might be exactly right, or he might be totally wrong, and usually, the reality is somewhere in the middle. That's his view of the experience. His partners might see themselves as victims just as much as he did and say that they invested money and effort and they had to throw it all away because he didn't have money or didn't want to put more money into the business. There are always two sides to the story—regardless, this is what he tells people.

The moment he does that, he **rationalizes** the story and **legitimizes** the story because when he talks about these things many times, he begins to believe them more and more. He also becomes good at telling that story and answering certain questions people might have.

Because he continues to repeat the story, he now believes it, and his brain is trained to see the situation through that story he's been telling. He's **fixated** on it.

The chances of him "divorcing" from the story he's now married to are slim. He's already committed to it. He can't go back to all of those people and tell them that he exaggerated or that he thinks he might have been wrong. He loses **motivation** to step out of that story, and now he lives his life through that scope of him being the victim of that story. He is comfortable with his version of the story, so in the future his brain will i try to prevent him from getting into another situation like that because it's trying to "protect" him from experiencing the pain in that past story.

Finally, I want to end with something I hear during 90% of my coaching calls, in one variation or another: "That's just the way I am." Sometimes it'll come in another variation like, "I never do these things," or "I've never done it in the past, so it's so not me that's the problem."

When I hear those types of statements, this screams to me, and hopefully to you after you read this book – "**MISSED OPPORTUNITY**" for growth.

Your personality is not set in stone, your destiny can and will be changed when you change the actions you make. More comfortable actions are just a tendency—you're not limited to any type of particular way of thinking, feeling or acting, and there is no reason why your actions should repeat the same as before. You shouldn't be committed to one way of approaching life or behaving.

The person you decide you want to become at the end of this book, the way people would talk about you and see you as an entrepreneur in the digital marketing space, doesn't and isn't around the traits you have. It's what you decide to do with your traits, the direction you choose to take, that sets leaders apart from those who would rather tuck their tail and avoid conflict or discomfort by running the other way.

People in the Industry Are Smart – Do Not Try to Fool Them

I've seen people who go and work for media, SaaS, and brands inside the industry, and I've seen people who create their own business as an affiliate, a brand owner, agency owner, or a network.

For some of them, manipulation and lying are the way they choose to interact with people.

The choice to act this way might be because this is their background. It could be because of the last place or industry they've worked or just because this is their personality, they like to exaggerate, lie, or just make up and embellish stories to include things that didn't really happen, didn't exist, or didn't play out exactly the way they claim.

To those people I always say: do not try to fool or lie to

anyone from the industry. The successful people in this industry are so smart that 99% of the time lies or exaggerated stories are going to backfire and hurt you.

Most of the time, these people either think they are smarter than other people or they think that because another person is quiet when they talk it's because they are eating their bullshit, instead of looking at the facts. Others do not want to be around people like this or work with them on any project...and the ones who do are just like them. They try and double down on the same mistakes that got them there.

Successful professionals in the industry have to juggle lots of people, lots of deals, plenty of situations where you have to think quickly and do many negotiations on a daily basis. They are extremely smart and experienced. Even the ones who are not as smart within the industry are likely to be extremely smart when compared to the general population.

I've seen these people who sell courses that are mediocre at best and people who claim to have "the best proven method" that will "make you money while you sleep, guaranteed." I've sat next to them at speaker engagements at conferences where I've spoken. Believe me, it doesn't take a degree in human psychology to understand that they know they're not being genuine to say the least, and I keep wondering, *Okay, this is working on the noobs, the amateurs that still didn't get scammed, but what about the rest of the industry?* There's absolutely no way a skilled and experienced digital marketer would want to do business with someone like that, unless they want to scam, too, and how is that a sustainable method?

Keep in mind, the lie is going to come out, sometimes it takes years, and then you start to see articles about an ongoing investigation on that person or the results of an investigation. Their name and how they're being perceived should be of more value to them than anything else. Another way to look at it is that you gain nothing from exaggerating, as you most likely need numbers to back it up at the end of the day, real numbers, unless those numbers do not hold up.

When attending conferences, or just when meeting people, whether in the affiliate marketing industry or in general, you'll come across plenty of people referred to as being "the biggest" in their field. You're going to hear that from a lot of people. Sometimes it will be true but remember this: Keep an eye open for people who dramatize their words or create impressions that seem to be more imaginative rather than based on anything real. I'm not saying you should completely dismiss working with them but *do consider this behavior a caution sign* and be extra careful.

A great way for me to recognize these people is by using a basic rule in poker—when someone has a **weak** hand, they'll act **strong** and when someone has a **strong** hand, they'll act **weak**. That rule usually applies and works within any human interaction, and when you learn to read it over time—when you're able to distinguish between the real persona and an act that covers up something else—things will become more transparent.

Looking at the younger audience flooding the industry nowadays, I see that it's growing more difficult due to the prevailing need to exhibit a "flexing" mentality. This involves showcasing your store's earnings and your numbers, and I just don't buy into it. Also, why would anyone choose to work with you, as a future partner or as an agency, when all you focus on is sharing your earnings figures online?

How can someone who is so into sharing and posting all the time be able to function at a high level?

Would you choose a partner that flexes and shows off all the time? It's not a good look.

I'm not here to tell you who you need to be, and I am certainly not the normal authentic standard, nor do I provide all the truth regarding how people should act. Everyone has their strengths—people attract and like people who are like them— and if you act like a show-off, you attract people who like this fake/flex/IG mentality. Is that really the type of people you want in your life?

The types of people who are so into displaying and bragging about what they have by flexing could've instead been investing back into the business or doing better things with their time and money.

Or others might perceive you as someone you're really not if you're too interested in bragging and showing off. Think about it. I recommend you dial it back and adopt a strategic, long-game perspective.

When you play the long game, you **create value**. This might sound cliche, but life is long (we can hope), which means you'll have a long career. Don't burn it all on a short play that really comes from greed or insecurity.

SIX

CREATING HIGH VALUE / SELF-BRAND / PERCEPTION

Also known as DHV (demonstration of high value), creating value is crucial for thriving. However, I would even argue that you need it to survive in business in general.

Demonstrating high value and building your own profile allows you to find the greatest unfair advantages you can have in the business:

1. Working with the more impressive people or companies in the industry, because they are going to take you more seriously.
2. Using the best materials available on your campaigns, like pre-landers/audiences/creatives, because when people see this, they are going to want to work with you. They can tell you'll be able to understand what's working and know what the specific needs are.
3. Finding the best affiliate manager, because affiliate networks are going to prioritize people they see as having better potential strategic partnerships.

4. Getting the best payment terms, because they value you and want to make it easier on you.
5. Arguing less with people about technical stuff, because they'll perceive you as an expert, and they'll believe you know what you're talking about.
6. Making the appropriate, sensible investments in what you need. Networks and advertisers will be able to invest more in what you need even before making money, because they'll see you as a strategic partner and therefore an excellent investment.

Defusing Lower Value Situations

If, by mistake or by circumstance, you get into a relationship where you are perceived to be of lower value, you're going to feel it right away. The way people treat you will come across differently. The number of people listening to what you have to say or how much you're being taken seriously is going to have a direct effect on you personally and business wise, you'll encounter loss of confidence in yourself. Some of the ways you'd notice these differences include the way some people speak with a lower tone or others stop speaking to you at all. The energy and vibe shifts, and you're not going to feel like yourself. I argue, and it's my experience, that if you're making a deal under those circumstances, this impression of low value HAS TO BE defused.

Examples of lower value situations

1. Going into business with someone you do not know or have not yet built a rapport with, they probably aren't aware of your accomplishments and they might consider you of a lower value depending on how they see you, where they are positioned in the deal, or how you come across. A relatable situation might be if you are going into business with two people—someone you know and someone you do not know who was brought into the deal by that person you know. Your

partner knows both of you, but you only know one person and that person also might "test" you, just like in the wild.

2. You go into business with someone who knows you from your past, before you went into business and evolved into who/what you are today. They know the old you and treat you like the former, less confident, you.
3. Some people will test you at the beginning, like if someone shouts at you or commands you to do something and you do not respond by asking them to respect you, this could create a lower value and hurt you as a brand and their perception of you.
4. You could also not be at fault and the other person is just a jerk that needs to be the center of attention all the time and wants to step on other people. Especially in those situations, you have to take control and be responsible for yourself. There's always a way forward.

Unless this is diffused, you'll face many challenges and losses:

1. It will take longer for you to make sure your business partner accepts any idea you have for the business, because they'll trust you less.
2. Their attitude will seep into how their employees perceive you and treat you.
3. In a situation where the business relationship hits a rock, or the company has to eliminate a partner, you may end up being the person who is let go.
4. Your day-to-day work will be judged and criticized in a way that shows further disrespect.

The 10-15 rule

The 10-15 rule is something I came up with myself and I'm pretty proud of. I created the concept to protect myself from going into deals I'm not supposed to get into and people I'm not supposed to go into business with. It's designed to remind me not to repeat the same mistakes over and over.

How it works is simple. Let's say you have a meeting with someone, and you show up on time, regardless of whether it's on Zoom or a physical meeting, and they don't show up on time. If you have a real interest in that meeting—meaning you want to sell them on something, you work for them, they are your client, or you want them to be—**you wait up to 15 mins**. After that, **you leave,** and they have to reschedule the meeting.

If **they asked for the meeting,** or essentially you are the one being sold to, **you wait up to 10 minutes** in that case.

I love the 10-15 rule because it makes it extremely easy way to:

1. Test someone's integrity for any type of business and filter out issues you might have in the future.
2. Create high value for yourself, and the chance to communicate your value to others.

The only exception is when they ask you for more time or say that they are going to be late, as long as that does not happen consistently with them.

Why is this rule so effective?

It's as effective as it is simple. It keeps you from being late to meetings because you can't follow that rule unless you are on time, every time, except when you communicate it in a direct way. If someone has stopped their work to meet with you and decided to give you their time, they're giving you pure respect, and if you're late, it's both disrespectful and counterproductive. If you're meeting with someone who works for you, each minute they wait for you is a minute they could be productive to your business.

I personally arrive at every meeting at least 10-15 minutes early. Why? Because life happens, and I don't want to view myself as a casual late arriver. It also shows the same character and respect that I demand in return from everyone with whom I work.

The primary reason for its effectiveness is rooted in simple logic: if someone doesn't value your time enough to inform you about their lateness or lacks good reasons for consistent tardiness, it's best to steer clear of doing business with them. If they show these at this initial stage, there's a strong likelihood they will only get worse over time.

By the way, this also applies to people who cannot leave their phones off for more than five minutes during a meeting. People who have to check their messages all the time are as disrespectful as those who are chronically late. It negates the whole purpose of the meeting and sends a direct message that the person who checks their messages has decided their time is much more important than yours.

SEVEN

YOU'RE THE BIGGEST BRAND YOU'LL EVER MANAGE

Congrats, you're already a brand owner—whether or not you knew it till now…and whether you like it or not. This is your new reality.

Essentially, you have managed **your own brand** for as long as you've been alive. Just like any other brand, you had some success and some failures. Some people have liked you, and some didn't (not that a good brand is necessarily built or based on the amount of people who like you). Building a brand in this industry—or really in any industry—when you're just starting out or in general is extremely important and is a key part of pushing yourself forward. As the industry grows bigger, as more agencies, more affiliate networks, and more brands compete, only the strong and bigger, better, recognizable brands will survive. That's just how it is.

If I told you to open up a podcast back in 2015 and you had invested your time in it, it could have become extremely popular by now. Today, it's much harder to start a podcast and gain traction, just like so many other situations. Bitcoin, the stock market, the largest litigation offices you know, the biggest hotel chains, they all started a long time ago and have built themselves up over the years.

It's always easier at the beginning of a trend. The ones who stick with it through the tough times rather than hoping to make quick money or who are fast-profit driven are also the ones who are going to make it in the long-run. Just like accumulating "likes" on Facebook or "followers" on Instagram, people who demonstrate ongoing commitment are the ones who succeed. That doesn't mean that right now it's impossible, it just means that you have to adopt and modify your strategy according to what's working right now generally and for you personally.

Here are some key rules I've applied throughout my branding journey. Some I discovered myself and others I learned from other people and implemented them in my life. These guidelines have had a tremendous effect of how others perceive my brand.

Managing YOU As a Brand

1. Be direct, and act with integrity.
2. Always end a relationship as well as you can.
3. Be nice. The number of people I've seen change after making money is crazy. They walk around acting superior and domineering after their success goes to their heads. Don't be that person, that's not the brand you want.
4. Make an effort, put your knowledge out there, and help people without expecting anything in return (at least not an immediate one). As the Bible says, "Cast thy bread upon the waters, for thou shalt find it after many days." In simpler terms, make every effort possible, and you will ultimately see a return.

This particular rule has to be one of the biggest ROIs I've ever had. Everything I do, from my YouTube channel to my decision not to sell any courses as well as to my speaking engagements—even when I had to take a 16-hour transatlantic flight to conferences that paid me a lot of money to be at twice a month—was built on a foundation of not asking for anything from the audience.

The people and opportunities I came across along the way were so important and made me so much money that it made me a believer in never expecting anything in return, but being grateful when it comes. I know and believe this mindset works so well that when someone talks to me at a conference, I would come to know quickly, in my mind, that it would only be a matter of time till we worked and generated money together.

Now, let's be real. I know many of you could not spend tens of thousands of dollars on travel expenses just to give away free knowledge and speeches. I know you need to work and make money, and I also understand you can't spend all your time helping people. You need to decide where and what you can do, and the level to which you can authentically help others. If you do come up with an idea that gives you great success, eventually share it. People are going to learn about it anyway, they might as well learn it from you and remember that you were the one who taught them.

And when I say *"authentically,"* I'm referring to the time you carve out amid your work commitments, kids, and maybe a mortgage. This is time dedicated to creating something, whether it's a course or a book, whether it's helping someone or filming videos or sharing your knowledge. Remember not to tell yourself those self-imposed and self-limiting narratives such as that that they already know this information, or that you're not a big enough player yet to share your knowledge. In fact, by doing these things, you elevate your status and become that bigger player because sharing knowledge expands your brand's reach and exposure to a broader audience.

. . .

Remember, this industry can be a rollercoaster ride. Sometimes you're going to need people and vice versa. There's no reason to not be nice, generous and approachable to everyone, and that even starts with how fast you answer messages, from people you know or strangers. Always be approachable. Even Elon Musk answers people privately on X.

Respect

Dominos isn't the best pizza, but they always get it on time and fast, and that's a big part of its success. Just like ordering pizza from a place you know that's going to deliver on time, you, as an affiliate, want to know you're going to get paid on time and they, affiliate networks or advertisers, want to know they have stability, with traffic...but not just traffic, they want to know that if they text you, you're going to respond fast. Both sides need stability. Revenue and scale aren't everything.

Respect isn't something you take, it's something you're given, and I've encountered different situations where people felt like "taking" respect would be the best approach.

For example, one of the repeating themes I've been hearing about and experiencing is that if you don't answer someone promptly, you can't be surprised when they give you the cold shoulder or end your connection.

I once sent an email to a big client. They wanted to renegotiate the deal we had because when we started, they didn't think we were going to scale or be as profitable as we became, and we never capped the percentage of the profits I earned from the deals. So, they were surprised when we scaled and reached big numbers (later in this book we'll talk about appropriately pricing a client). I gave them a few points on where they stood, and they didn't reply for five days. The first chance I had, during the start of the team meeting, I asked them if they received my email and when they planned on responding. Later they wrote me an angry email about how I'd dared to ask about my correspondence at the start of a company Zoom meeting, and that it was unprofessional, and they were pissed about it.

While I fully understand that some people may see my communication style as me "coming at them" or that this was, in some eyes, an unprofessional move, they also deserve to have their own interpretation of the situation. They also have their 50% stake in our contract—why would they wait five days without even acknowledging the fact that they were sent an email by one of their biggest contractors? Delaying communications certainly didn't serve their interest. Even if they didn't know how to respond, or even if they just didn't have the time, why not just send back a short email that they received my message and they'd come back with an answer soon? This was not an unusual way of interacting with this specific client, that's just the way they reacted to everyone. So, when they responded by acting offended, I wasn't surprised on one hand, but still a bit in shock because they shot themselves in the foot by delaying a renegotiation.

Demanding respect in return, after **failing to give respect** to the person who initially emailed you, is puzzling. A basic indication of respect is replying to an email saying that you received it and you'll schedule a call—this should've been enough. Yet, this person decided that he was superior, and that people owe him. While I as his contractor do owe him something, his angry response and lack of respect didn't work to his advantage, when he wants and needs to keep the best relationship he could have with me, and me with him.

Being willing to draw a clear line or walk away from a relationship where there's a demonstrated lack of respect should always be an option. Don't get me wrong, if someone crosses a boundary and you still believe fighting for them or the relationship is worthwhile, that could be a smart option.

But if you want respect from the affiliate network, client, or contractor you're dealing with, you first have to be respectful of them, their time, and what they need and want. This is regard-less of who pays who, or who needs who, and yes, even who works for whom. Why? Because if both parties are content, there's more to gain. The contractor/client or employee is going to give more, stay longer and care more when he's happy with the relationship. Again, while the default way to approach a situation should not go towards escalating it, you want to have that weapon as a legitimate tool to be used whenever you need it.

When someone demands to be respected, they lose credit, they don't get credit. Demanding respect is a weak move, not a strong one, and when you disrespect someone whom you work with, at the end of the day you disrespect yourself, even if you don't acknowledge it.

EIGHT
BUILDING A MULTI-LEGGED CHAIR

This industry has so many options on one side and on the other—and strong opinions everywhere you turn—it can seem very unstable.

As a Capricorn, I like having as much stability as possible, and that's what I suggest you do when you start building your strategy. Nothing moves the way you want it to move throughout long periods of time if you don't build that strategy that's going to lead you to your goals. When you have no strategy, best case scenario is you're going to be stuck with only one method of operation, scared shitless if it shuts down for some reason.

While a lot of people in the industry are focused on one specific project, product, or service, a good idea would be to try to create several sources of revenue for your single operation or just a few different revenue channels through multiple projects. If you're looking for stability and scale, this is a must.

One way to do this, for example, could be managing a few brands, services, and businesses within the industry. With the right structure, that could be a smart move.

Another way could be taking that one single thing you do and making sure that you don't only run traffic but also become a network for other affiliates and make some profits out of what they bring in.

Do you have an agency? A creative team? Great. Try to build a direct-to-consumer (DTC) brand.

Are you an affiliate? Running offers and sending traffic to affiliate networks? Try building an offer.

Are you into building a DTC brand? Try to also set up a small agency on the side.

And even if you're focused on one specific thing, diversify within that focus. If you have a DTC brand, recruit affiliates and affiliate networks for traffic and don't rely just on your campaigns.

If you have an agency, try investing in clients where you want to get a stake in their businesses.

These are just examples of your options. The cliché is true: putting all of your eggs in one basket is a risky move. At the end of the day, it's not worth doing that because you could invest the same resources in one service or company and still make another project or service on the side with the right structure.

Need more ideas?

Here are two more:

1. Get as many quality employees as you can and delegate your daily tasks to them. When this is stabilized you can invest your time into the new operation. If you want to "scale" that idea even more, build a more sophisticated structure where you have captains in charge of specific businesses that manage more than the day-to-day logistics of that business and have them recruit and delegate their tasks to employees.

2. Find someone who's into a certain field, who might be working at a company that's doing what you want to do and create a business with them. If you have capital, then risk your money and let them get the

operation up for both of you - joining only when it really gets up. That allows you to keep full control over your current operations while not investing time in getting a new operation up and running. This way you're setting up multiple operations so that even if one of them fails, you still make up the money you initially invested.

- This is a bullet-proof method as it holds the key to smart investing or Asymmetric Investing, meaning that your bet or investment has a potential upside in a position that is much greater than its potential downside. If you risk $1,000 for the chance of making $10,000, you make an asymmetrical bet. If you risk $1,000 for the chance of making $1,000, you make a symmetrical bet.
- Here, the plan is to create businesses that could make a lot of money over a long period of time, and so, it's enough that only one of them would actually create profit for you to make a profit on all of them.

Some people who read this chapter or this part of the book might say that they simply do not agree, and you should focus on only one thing. They might be right because that's what worked for them or people they know—that's why they are big believers in focusing on one specific option. It's completely okay to think that way, and at the end of the day if that's what is working for you that's amazing. I've seen people do the same thing for years and years and it was stable for them and working. But considering all the changes that have happened over the past 10 years, for me it's just unnerving to think that I'm dependent on only one source of traffic or one source of revenue. I've experienced and heard too many stories where people thought something would continue going "for life," and when that came crashing down, they lost everything.

I also think that there's a lot of in-between here, meaning that there are not only two options—focus on one specific thing or succumbing to the "shiny object syndrome." There are numerous options between these two extremes, and that's what's beautiful about entrepreneurship. There are multiple avenues to success.

NINE

THE IMPORTANCE OF MASTERMINDS, MEETUPS AND CONFERENCES

I cannot stress enough the importance of these three elements are and how enriching and fun they can be when used and approached effectively (we'll discuss how to make effective use of them in this chapter). The number of people, including myself, who closed life changing deals and partnerships, and strengthened existing relationships is huge. It's not just amateur players who attend these. Seasoned pros are also making strong new connections and gain fresh insights in the industry. Given the rapid evolution of this field, there's always something new to learn or someone new to meet.

I haven't been to a lot of other industry conferences, but I wouldn't be surprised if those conferences are way more conservative, slow, and mature…in a bad way.

The masterminds and conferences in the affiliate marketing and digital marketing space—from the smaller, more intimate ones to the bigger ones—are fast, full of young, energized people, and exciting.

The big upside is that they are a lot more interesting and vibrant. Sometimes it doesn't feel so corporate or has no corporate feel at all, which is freeing. You don't have to wear a suit to the conference, and the communication is much more direct, young, and fresh. The downside is that you could be drawn to the intense, fast-paced "affiliate lifestyle"—which can include drugs, partying all night, etc. People who come from other industries could have a hard time adjusting since they don't realize they are talking to individuals who can make a lot of fast money while not knowing how to manage it yet. The vibe is completely different. Making money when you're younger is completely different than making it when you're older, and for older people these conferences could look like they came straight out of the *Wolf of Wall Street* movie.

I had a talk with a friend, and I tried explaining to him that when you go to a conference everything is super quick. You have up to 72 hours to really understand what's going on and how to maximize your time. You'll meet so many people. Who is someone you want to partner with? Who's just a talker? Who is a liar? Who do you trust and who do you stay away from? It's intense and exhausting, and that's the case regardless of whether you're jet-lagged or just tired from traveling to the conference.

The more experienced players are doing it much faster than 72 hours. By the time 24 hours or less have passed they've scanned the room, talked to almost everyone they wanted to, and categorized everyone. They came goal-oriented and have a memory system in place so they can make use of the information they've gathered later on. Those skills take time, so you can't expect to be like that at the beginning. Much experience cannot be learned from a book; you have to get boots on the ground.

That friend told me that he doesn't understand why people take it so seriously, and why someone has to spend so much brain resources and energy around something that should be easy and fun.

He said, "Well, I'll just talk to someone and take it one conversation at a time."

That friend likes soccer, so I gave him a soccer analogy.

I told him, "Sure you could go on the attack and every time

you get the ball—you're just focused on how to score. That's not a bad approach to playing the game, but it's a very narrow one."

If you're playing the game at a high level and want to maximize the time you're there and the number of possible situations, then you want to be Messi: one of the best players out there. When Messi goes on the field, he's not only ready and trained, he's also well prepared and has done background work on the other team. He knows who they played in the last couple of games. He knows if they won, and who they're playing next. Are some players having trouble in their personal lives that might possibly impact their game? Are we playing on our home field or outside of it?

All these thoughts and questions could translate to attending a conference. Is that person traveling from out of the country? Is he jetlagged? Does he usually talk a lot or have short conversations? Is he someone you can rely on? Is he cheating on his wife during the conference? Is he using drugs? What do other people who've worked with him say about him? Do you know anyone who has worked with him before? Is he the center of attention?

My friend said that dealing with all of that might be too much for anyone, and I answered, "That may be true." What I told him, I'll also tell you—if you're goal-oriented and want to maximize the results you're getting at every conference, consider that time is your most valuable asset, and that time is also extremely limited at these types of events. There's really no other option than **mapping, categorizing** and **memorizing** each person you meet, while **limiting** every interaction you may have at an event.

Let me start from the end: **limiting** each interaction is important because there are several people you want to meet, and you want those meetings to be high quality. Whether you like it or not, your time and energy are running out every second you're at a venue. Another reason why limiting interactions should be a priority is because of positioning and the perceived value (or the branding you're creating for yourself).

Let me dig a bit deeper into these ideas.

When people teach strategies for improving network skills, many techniques and approaches to navigating networking events or conferences emerge. One rule people often learn is the three-seconds rule, which emphasizes that when you first have an interaction with someone, or even share a look with them, you have a very short period of time to act before that person starts associating negative traits to you. They might think you're not as confident and you should be to do business with them or not as smart as someone they would want by their side.

Another approach would be making sure you never ask for that person's contact information, especially if they expect you to, or even offer to work together, but you don't. That makes them think you are of a higher value, that you have too much work, or are too much in demand, and they will consciously or subconsciously want to work with you more.

People *subconsciously* don't appreciate you when you give them the feeling you have all the time in the world to talk to them. Sure, on the surface they enjoy the attention you're paying them and might think you're a great person. But in this book, we're not going for great, we're going for the superstar results. That's on the spectrum between being liked and "feared" that we'll talk about later in this book.

Among those I coach, a common strategy for overcoming tasks they don't like to do or tend to delay doing is setting up meetings or agreeing to meet someone at a certain hour of the day. However, when they create a specific timeframe to accomplish an activity, they know they have limited time in which to work, so they must be efficient and effective.

Taking this idea one step further, imagine a life where people don't die. Would you agree that people would be a lot less effective and there would be more people slacking off in the world? Knowing our time is limited enhances our awareness of the time we have in this world. Sure, sometimes we forget that we're only here temporarily, and yes there are a lot of people in this world who go through life not thinking about those limits. But accepting this finite reality and using it to your advantage is beneficial.

When you **limit** each conversation, you get to the point much faster and that person, whether they understand it or not, would perceive you as having **higher value**. I can't stress how important this is, from getting you much greater chances of actually doing business with that person, to improving your position in a negotiation situation in terms of leverage. If that person is looking to do business with the best (and who isn't?) and has multiple options, you'll at the very least land a little above anyone else.

I've seen people being given equity in big, profitable companies, purely because of their ability to create the perception of higher value.

How do you do it? Communicate it at the very start of any interaction. You could say something like: "Yes, let's talk. I have another meeting in fifteen minutes so we can talk now." Or if the conversion already started, and it looks like you want to engage more with this person, you could say something like: "I have to be at another call/meeting in ten minutes, and I want to make the most out of our initial talk. Let's schedule a longer meeting when I return." This is a good idea regardless of whether you have other meetings because it helps remove that small talk and gets them get to the point faster. With the connection established, the call will be more effective and efficient.

The last thing I want to emphasize here is *how* you request a future meeting. Be aware of the line between coming across as a douchebag with an ego bigger than the room versus a person who just values his time and has many people wanting to do business with him. When you communicate with the other person, make sure you are being respectful. Most of all, you must sound and feel authentic about wanting to talk to them later, even though you don't have the time right now.

For those of you who do not know the **7-38-55 Rule**: this rule talks about how only **7%** of all communication is done through verbal communication, whereas the non-verbal component of our daily communication, such as the tone of our voice and body language, make up **38%** and **55%** respectively. The sound of your voice or a light encouraging tap on the shoulder could change how you're perceived by the other person.

Remember, conferences aren't made for longer meetings in general—unless you cherry picked specific people you're already in contact with/doing business with, or you actually decided to close a deal there. Our goals at conferences are to meet, network, communicate, leave a good impression, and set up a longer meeting for after the event. That's how you maximize the number of interactions you have and increase your chances of making more deals later on. Going deep into a conversation or a deal is something you could do when you're back home— meeting new people isn't. Your time at the conference is limited, or more limited than your time back at the office or home.

The best hunters in the wild move quickly. They have a strategic plan. They have a specific goal or list of goals. They know the specific outcome that would follow if they achieved that goal, and they have a perfect or near perfect system to help them make quick decisions and remember everything that is going on. They use this system and their memory to achieve better results each time they take an action.

Mapping is the initial strategy I mentioned above.

As you scan a conference room, start by dividing people inside a conference hall into three groups.

1. People who don't know where they are going (physically) next – the stage, another booth, or they would just follow someone else.
2. People who are just looking for people to talk to that they know.
3. People who are focused on meeting others, recruiting affiliates and/or working in sales.

What's interesting is that the people in Group 3 who work at scheduling future meetings and networking usually make the least amount of money, because they usually work for a company and not for themselves. Yet they get to know the most people and are usually the most goal oriented. There are two reasons for that: first, they have a strategy; second, they are goal oriented. They know exactly what they want to extract from this situation in the time they are there.

A part of the reason this happens is that they have a boss, and they need to show specific results. People who work for themselves tend to forget that there's a direct correlation between the strategy and the number of people you meet at events and the amount of money you could potentially make.

So **mapping** is about having a specific schedule and strategy for what you're going to do, starting with who you're going to try to connect with at the venue, when you're going to go, and who you'll see talking onstage.

Will you be going booth by booth to visit all the companies? Is there anyone specific you're looking to see?

Remember that when you have a strategy in place and specific people you want to meet, your brain is going to automatically look for them.

When you come across someone and have a casual conversation, **categorizing** is all about the time it takes you to understand who that person is, where they are in their career, how you could help them and how they could benefit you. Are they just looking to recruit you as an affiliate, or could they be your next potential partner?

Keep in mind that a person who isn't relevant now could become relevant later. Don't outright dismiss a connection you make, especially if it's a good one. They could be working for someone now and become an entrepreneur later, for example, opening up the door for you to do business together. Your current conversation is just planting the seed, nothing needs to come out of it right this moment, and this is something to keep in mind every time you network.

Categorizing is the only effective way I know of processing a large number of people effectively, at least at the beginning of every interaction you have with any person. This is often a method used for security purposes at a lot of airports around the world.

One of the ways that I use it relies on a famous poker player's way of categorizing according to animals, colors, or anything that would help you remember. I personally do it by astrological signs, because that's what helps me remember people. The key is that when you associate someone with something else to help you remember them, it becomes a lot faster to understand if you should spend time talking with them...and how much time.

When you become very good at quickly categorizing, and you want to take it to the next level, you can do so by creating a specific list of questions and filters to go by. This might change based on the person or what you're trying to achieve. Here are some questions you can use as filters to discern the value of your connection:

- Are you working for a company, or do you work for yourself right now?
- Are you potentially looking to open a new business with someone you meet?
- What types of markets interest you?
- What is your unfair advantage?

You could also categorize that person by how interesting they are and how smart or authentic you think they are or the best option - according to the goals you've set at the beginning of the conference.

Memorizing would be the last, crucial part you need to know about. This system must be put in place in order for everything to connect. If you don't have it, nothing that you did prior would matter, you're not going to remember anyone, and you would have just wasted your time.

It took me so long to perfect something that works for me, and before then I used to go to conferences and maybe follow up on 10% of my interactions. Looking back, I can't even imagine how much money I potentially lost.

Some people take a selfie with that person they have just met. Some people write inside the chat box the topics they have talked about with that person. There are many ways to do it, and you have to figure out what works for you.

Let me summarize this by saying that it's going to take time for you to get better at this. At the beginning, you're going to make mistakes when it comes to time management, strategy, and decisions about how to spend your time...or even which people you are going to meet or do business with. Just like everything else in life, some things just require more experience so don't be hard on yourself when it comes to the learning process. The fact that you know about and can rely on this roadmap or cheat sheet puts you ahead of most of the field, and I wish I had developed this back when I started.

It just takes time to adjust to the shift of being a professional networker, understanding that unlike what you are used to up till now, the fact that you have traveled to a conference does not mean that you're on vacation or that it should be based on fun, shopping, partying, etc. This takes me back to what I said earlier in this book—in a world where you have to choose between two types of suffering, one of discipline and integrity and one of regret, I highly recommend choosing discipline.

I'm not saying you shouldn't have fun, but just like when you're following a diet, you're going to have moments where you want to eat everything in front of you and you forget about your goals. It's important to train yourself not to lose it in those moments.

· · ·

Conferences:

When you go to conferences, never ask, "What do you do?" It's like asking a beautiful girl or handsome guy, "Want to date me?" The industry is about supply and demand, if someone is hot/a stud, you need to engage them, just like you would with a high-demand boy or girl you want to date.

And just like in the dating world, the people you're with and places you visit will help you get to higher tier people. So, walking with an entourage/herd is often an advantage.

I love the quote from *Ozark*, I think it's in the first episode: "Money is not peace of mind. Money is not happiness. Money is, at its essence, that measure of a man's choices."

Essentially, your bank account reflects the decisions you make in life. It's somewhat inevitable.

Every decision you're making, regardless of whether it has to do directly with business or not, still impacts (directly or indirectly) the number that is showing on your bank account.

If you divorce, that will be reflected at some level when you log in to your bank account. If you choose a business partner who ends up using drugs, that could highly impact your bank account.

Everything you do results in either a higher or lower amount of money in your bank account... On the other hand, maintaining the current amount you have now is just like losing money, not just because of inflation but also because every business that does not progress, expand, and grow goes backward, and that's just reality.

The number of deals I saw going wrong or being canceled, and the number of opportunities that were lost just because someone was acting up at an event is so big, it's crazy. Those problems could have easily been avoided, and they were mistakes or decisions that were non-business related like drinking too much or overusing drugs, but they still affected how people saw those individuals, their brand, and bottom line. Their bank accounts.

I have so many examples of people who were just about to close multiple deals and partnerships, and also planned to continue speaking at conferences, but they were using so many drugs or drinking so heavily that when people saw them at the conference, they decided they might not be the stable partner they are looking for.

And that brings me to this point: a conference is not a party. You are not abroad with your friends from high school or college. These are your potential partners, employers, or advertisers that you are going to send traffic to. Remember that every decision you make will impact your pocket at the end of the day.

The reason I love this sentence is that at the end of the day, you can't really make the numbers lie. They are there in front of you in black and white. The game is not how much you're loved by everyone. The game is not how much everyone loves to party or drink with you. Every sports game has a score at the end. Ours, in business, is ROI and the bank statement, basic as that may sound.

You could say I'm overthinking this, some would even say I'm paranoid, but ignoring these stories that I keep seeing repeated—and thinking that you're the only one that takes mental-notes and remembers how others behave at a conference —is probably even more strange.

To make the best use of your time at a conference or a mastermind:

Ask if you can access replays of the talks and knowledge that's being shared at that specific event—and if you do, and it's free— only go to at most 10% of the talks. Of those 10%, focus on the ones that hold real significance for you, the ones you absolutely believe are going to push you forward. Maybe you already know or heard of that speaker in the past. The main reasons for spending your time listening to a talk at a conference are the following:

1. You're exhausted from talking to people and want to rest.
2. You want to talk to the speaker later and you want to have context when you do.
3. You feel like the knowledge/topic he/she is going to talk about would be crucial to your business or campaigns and waiting for replays might end up causing you to lose money by not implementing their methods.
4. You met someone at the conference, and you want to take time to hang with them and use that as a way of building rapport.

Remember, hearing/viewing the talks is something you can do from home. Meeting people is something you can't do at home, and this is coming from a person who has been a speaker at over 100 events as of writing this book. This is basic time management. Don't use the conference talks to run from networking.

Time and energy management are HUGE. Make sure you are well rested. Truth is, you don't have to be at the conference from the second it opens till the second they close the doors at the end of the night. If you know that you have dinner or an event waiting for you that evening and you're tired, make sure you sleep a little beforehand. Many people approach conferences like they're a sprint and they end up tired and drained. You want to be sharp and look sharp when you talk to people, not tired and slow. Instead, approach an event like a marathon, and take it at a steady pace that feels right for you.

Sometimes I would even leave the conference for a quick (or not quick) power nap because I know there's a lot more going on at night. You do not have to stay till the very last second. If you feel like you are maxed out, go and get some rest.

. . .

1. Stay away from long meetings. Make sure you limit meetings in terms of time and communicate this narrow timeframe to the other party when you meet her or him. Researchers say that the optimal time when the brain is functioning well is up to an hour, but closer to 30 minutes is even better. Long meetings can be scheduled when you are back home unless you really only came to meet with people you know and strengthen current relationships. There is no reason to meet for more than an hour unless you are also doing something fun like a dinner or another event.

2. Be goal oriented. Ask yourself before even purchasing tickets to that event: *What do I want to get out of this event?* Write down your answers. Then for every minute you spend and every conversation you have, be sure to ask yourself: "Is this decision going to help me get close to the goals I've set for this conference?" If the answer is no, unless you've found out something really interesting and/or that list of goals changes (something that could happen during a conference to shift your experience or perspective) make sure that you stay away from or change a decision that doesn't align.

This is a good tool to determine why you really are going. I had a friend who started talking to me about the hotels he's going to book for the next conference he's planning to attend, and I asked him, "What are your plans for this one?" He said that he just has a free ticket from last time and that's why he's planning on going. I told him that it sounded like the reason for him showing up to this event is just the fact that he has a free pass, and if he didn't have one, he would probably never purchase one. If that's the case, he shouldn't go to the event because it's such a useless reason to attend.

Always ask yourself the "why" even before the goal-setting phase.

The Dos and Don'ts at a Conference – Recap:

1. Look clean and sharp. I can't be more blunt about this: Make sure you shower. This isn't another zoom meeting. I could also tell the people who'd been sleeping two seconds before they took the elevator downstairs to the conference, and they walked around the whole day looking rumpled and unkempt. Excellent hygiene is paramount to making a positive first impression.

2. This is not the time to try new things. If you're usually not a drinker, if you usually don't eat a lot or don't work out, if you usually don't go on rollercoasters— this is NOT the time to try it for the first time. You don't get this networking opportunity every day. When you do, you want to take advantage of it as much as you can, not spend the time puking in your room. Play it safe, try these things at home with your friends first.

3. One of my biggest no-no's when it comes to conferences is getting into a long conversation with someone, unless it comes with the right context beforehand.

Let me explain. Even if that person wants to be in a long conversation with you, and believe me, as much as you may think they do, they are probably not into it as much as you are (to say the least), it's still the wrong decision on your part. As I mentioned previously, the whole purpose of the mastermind or conference is to reach your goals, the ones you're setting before each event you attend, and there's no way to meet these goals without time management and making sure you maximize your time. You're trying to get to know as many people as possible—the longer discussions and potential deal-making can wait for later, after the conference... It's a lead campaign essentially.

Those people who are getting into long discussions (20+ minutes) are making the same mistake as people who are trying to play their own music or the music that they love to hear when going into a party they are invited to. It's not good in terms of positioning, since the chances of someone making a deal with you later (when that person thinks you're very busy talking to so many other people at the conference) are just way higher.

So, we really have no reason to get into a long conversation with anyone, as interesting as they may be. You want to optimize the time and energy when you're at a conference, and the brain is the most energy consuming part we have. Let's keep it sharp and talk to as many people as possible.

Context is extremely important here, so let me give you an example. Do you know the feeling when someone you don't know well comes and hugs you or touches you? Or you're thinking of something negative or just not in the mood and someone comes into your space and gets too close? Then you're in a worse mood, and you want to push that person away.

Now just imagine you can't really know what that person feels like right now, so if you still are going for that longer conversation, make sure you do your homework beforehand, meaning you know him a bit more than someone you've just met at this conference. Maybe you saw that he usually talks longer than usual with people around him, but critically you want to get his permission to get into a longer discussion.

Every time I had a "dry season," or I was just looking for my next project or work opportunity, a good meetup or conference was usually all I needed. I got my motivation from them, removed any doubts going through my head, and found new connections that helped me push forward to the next level. But like I said, this is me. You need to find whatever works best for you, whatever pushes and motivates you.

A quote from the Bible reads, "A prophet is not without honor except in his own country," which means a person is respected everywhere except their own small group or inner circle. I suggest this can mean that you can't be the one that pushes you. Often, we need an outside stimulus or prompt to encourage us to take action.

Up to now we've talked about mindset, setting you up internally and creating the right base for you to build your persona and a stable business to scale profitably. But for you to become sharp as a wolf when it comes to understanding various situations at conferences and meetings, the next few chapters dig deeper into specific interactions you might have at conferences, and my examples will help you become apex strategists in business situations to extract the most out of them.

TEN
SELF-BRANDING

People become brands by appearing many times and achieving a lot of impressions, and at the end of the day what counts is how memorable they are. This is why you see very interesting characters in conferences and masterminds, wearing interesting shirts, different hats or mustaches, and similar facial expressions. These people probably have a certain style, and this is how they want to be seen or they think it looks nice on them, but a high percentage of them also know that in order to be remembered they have to look unique. I know of people being invited to speak just because their brand was so strong, even while their content wasn't particularly interesting.

To make an interesting analogy:

- If CPC (cost per click) x CVR (conversion rate) = CPA (cost per action/acquisition)
- Then, Impressions x How Memorable = Self-Branding or how strong your band is…and that is all under the

assumption that you are being memorable for good reasons and not for negative reasons.

We've all been in a room where there are a certain number of people (probably small) where everyone there will remember a particular person. Even those who don't recall that person's name will remember that individual when you mention the color of the shirt they wore or how they looked or something funny they said.

I can't stress it enough. Self-branding is critical to any career in order to attract more clients, more projects, and accelerate your career advancement.

Certain speakers are regularly at the largest events in the industry, invited to every place imaginable, doing back-to-back events. Whether or not they added or changed anything in their presentation in the past four years, it's irrelevant. The value they provide can be minimal, they can waste 50% of their time on stage talking about who they are and their history, **but** they still get invited because they are memorable.

If I had to guess, the main reason people try to blend in and fail at successfully self-branding is due to fear. Everyone has their own fears. Psychologists say that there are two common contributors to fears—the fear of not being loved and the fear of not being enough...not being smart enough, rich enough, funny enough.

Years ago, I went to a personal development retreat where we talked about a topic similar to this. The speaker there asked, "What do you think is the biggest motivation people have? What makes them choose certain decisions in life and pushes them forward, regardless of where they live or who they are?" The answer was: *what others say about you.* That's when I realized that people don't speak up, don't go on stage, and end up hiding their finest traits because they fear what others are going to say about them. Fear controls and undermines the success of so many people.

During that retreat I came to understand that it doesn't matter what you do, people are going to have an opinion and something to say about you.

So why not just stop caring what they say?

Why not just look at people talking about you as an indicator of a positive result, one that's on track to achieving advancement in your career?

People are going to talk about how you dress, how you look, how funny or not funny you are—regardless of whether you wear the most expensive thing or the cheapest thing, they're going to have something to say.

If you say something funny, some people are going to say, "That comment makes no sense, he's dumb." While others might say, "He's a fun person to hang with."

If you wear something expensive, some people are going to say, "She's showing off," while others are going to think you have style.

What I'm trying to explain is that it's kind of like the saying, "There is no bad advertisement." You would rather people talk positively *or* negatively about you rather than feel like you don't exist.

This is the part where someone usually tells me: "Yeah, Wolf, **but** you'd rather have them say good things and not bad things." In general, sure, that's true.

HOWEVER:

1. You can't control what anyone else says or thinks. You could mean one thing and they'll hear something else. I've encountered dozens of situations where I've genuinely tried helping someone and they were sure I was interacting in a way that would cause them harm.

2. I know lots of people who say really nice things about
   someone who no one wants to work with. Other times,
   people say terrible things about a person who rakes in
   money all day, so there isn't a direct correlation
   between good comments and an influx of money.

Get What You Want By Communicating It Directly

When you choose a partner to enter a new venture with, I suggest you verbally communicate your thoughts and fears—and if you don't have any, that's a sign that you're either too naive to get into the deal or that you're missing something that they didn't tell you. Your Spidey senses should be alert at all times.

Listen to the whispers early so you won't have to hear the screams later. In over 90% of cases where I heard people got scammed, entered a bad relationship, gave a loan to someone, or opened a business with someone they shouldn't have—whether with family or an acquaintance—more than 90% of the time the writing was on the wall in some form from the very beginning. Listen to those subtle signs and warnings.

Let me share a story with you. A new friend suggested that I get into his new DTC (direct to consumer) brand. We negotiated the equity and how things are going to work, and he was keen on getting started.

While we were finishing the last of the paperwork and final revisions of our contract, I started seeing that in the past three to four months, the guy wasn't really into working. He was investing more time in his Instagram stories than in any of his businesses, and I was afraid that he had a different approach to business than I did. He seemed to think he could get a lot of employees to do what he needed to do and then, from that point on, he wouldn't need to actually work. While my approach is way different and involves "boots on the ground" by all partners in the first months or even years of a business, until it is stable and takes off.

I communicated everything with him and told him that I was sure I could get this brand to where we want it, but we had to make sure that he was on it, not just putting employees or other people on it, and how could he do it while traveling all year long?

I don't know anyone who is able to function at a high level when their focus is in a different place.

I tried to explain that I'm not trying to criticize or want him to change on my behalf or handle the whole deal himself. It was just important to communicate it directly and make sure that we were on the same page. His DTC brand might still crush it and work really well. While there's more than one way of making things happen, his approach just wasn't the way I work.

I believe that this example conveys what I'm trying to explain here—many people can go into the deal, not thinking of what could happen and setting themselves and even the brand at risk, or they can just disappear and ghost the other person.

That's why I'm a big believer in communicating as directly as possible. That approach has never disappointed me. It saves time, money, and potential bad experiences.

How to Address Someone or Talk to Someone – Face-to-Face, on Social Media Platforms, Email or Writing

First of all, when you ask for someone's time, stop offering them a coffee or beer. Seriously.

Over the years, I've collected some do's and don'ts when it comes to messaging someone online or approaching someone at an event:

- Don't offer them coffee, a beer or a generic meeting where that person doesn't even know what the meeting is about.

- Don't send "hi/hey" messages. It only adds another layer of ambiguity to the communication. It's unhelpful, and the person you're sending this to is probably busy. Even if they are not, they might look at it as a waste of their time or, even worse, you're disrespecting their time.
- Don't write: "How are you?" / "How's it going?" for the same reasons.
- Don't write: "I'd love to chat with you over beer/coffee" – no one has time to "sit and chat" with you, it's just a turnoff.
- And absolutely don't ask questions that invade someone's privacy like, "When are you home?" "When do you get back?" "What are you doing now?" – these are the most hated questions for me by far.

Instead of the above missteps, you should create a template that you continue to refine indefinitely until you find what works best for you.

Here are a couple of structure ideas for you to use:

- Short intro > offer value > define goal > specific call to action

—OR—

- Hook intro > value > goal + call to action

Here's an example on how to use it:

"Hey, John! I hope everything is great. I'd love to talk to you about your email marketing experience. In the last few years, I've been working with multiple email experts and have managed to triple their business using my software that increases their inbox rate by 10%-25% on average.

"I'd appreciate the chance to go on a short video call for 15-20 minutes and see if we could generate money for each other and I could learn from your experience. If next week sounds good, I'd like to schedule a call."

Another example could be:

"Hey, John! I'm Maor and I've been a media buyer for big companies for the last 13 years. I usually don't approach or actively recruit clients, but the reason I'm writing to you today is because I had a client for a few years that is your direct competitor and I have a lot of experience with your specific niche and campaigns that are basically ready and that could save you money and give us a head start.

"I'd love to go on a short call to see if we could work together, and if we can't, just meeting would be great too! How's this week sound to you?"

The important things for me when writing a message like those are:

1. Not sounding too salesy. I want to make sure that the message is authentic and not too pushy.
2. Creating a short, intriguing experience. The goal is to make the recipient so interested that they can't sleep till they message me back. In the above example, they would likely be curious about their main competitor who I ran traffic to and improved their business.

This type of message might contain more text, yes, but it gives more information and context to the person that you're sending it to. There's enough information here for the person to decide if they want to spend their time on a call with me and allow them to prepare for this meeting.

The biggest upside to this method is that it gets you and the other person focused on what the call is going to be about by setting specific goals you want to gain from this call.

I'm not looking to take knowledge or time from you—I'm always looking to give first. That should be the mindset when writing any type of message.

Next, I'll talk about what happens after the initial attempt to engage. Sometimes, you'll inevitably face rejection.

ELEVEN
DEFUSING REJECTION

One of the best signs of positive interaction is that, just like any good high, it can also bring in a low, just like every A/C that creates cool currents indoors as well as heat on the other side.

If you successfully engage in an intriguing conversation, that person will likely send you a message back, at the very least. However, just like with every intriguing experience that draws a person into a conversation, various concerns could arise.

In conversations, much like the highs and lows of life, even if you manage to create an engaging conversation where you highlight positive things about yourself, your services, or the products you sell, leaving with a positive overall impression and a sense of the other person's focus and interest, there could also be downsides, such as potential concerns from the other side.

For example, a typical concern would be that the person thinks you're trying to scam them, or they worry that if the solution you're offering is generating so much money right now, why would you want to offer it to someone else?

In the example I gave in the last chapter, I wrote to the prospective client mentioning that I ran traffic to one of their direct competitors. That might really make them want to ask me who that was and get more information about their direct competitor's marketing strategy. On the downside that also might cause them to think that they shouldn't take me on and work with me because then I could revert back to their competitor or go to another competitor in the same field and do whatever I'm doing right now—even share their marketing strategy. They might think I'm not loyal.

In any case, you need to make sure you have a quick, satisfying, answer that makes sense and could defuse the situation when they ask about their questions/concerns.

Again, in this example, I could tell the client that I have been working for a few years with that competitor and the reason I decided to leave is that I wanted to do more to advance his company and he was holding me back. OR I could say something vague and show that I'm being respectful and that after a few years things weren't working out between me and that competitor (that shows that I was solid, and not just working with that client for a short period of time). I decided to cut the tie and move on.

When you're in this situation, you need to keep the conversation dynamic and prepare an answer that defuses the initial way you approached them. In order to catch the bigger fish or hook the people who are likely not going to answer just another random DM, you want to be prepared to respond appropriately, whether it's by baiting the hook or diffusing their concerns.

TWELVE
CREATING A PROFILING SYSTEM

When you attend a conference, you'll meet and engage with many people (if you're following my suggestions in this book). When you meet hundreds of people in a short timeframe, unlike a workspace or in your day-to-day life, you need to be able to distinguish various types of people.

If you're good at recognizing patterns, this is going to be easy for you, and if you're not, this is going to take a bit more energy —but it will allow you to recognize who's who faster and avoid certain people and situations that might rob you of your time, energy or even money if you decide to go into business with them.

If you look at any place where a large number of people are gathered, either because of security purposes or other state laws like going through customs, they often use profiling. In airports, they may profile according to racial or cultural classifications. At events, parties, and fancy nightclubs, they might profile according to how you look. These are effective systems for classifying large numbers of people at a glance. Yes, these methods have received a lot of criticism from different groups of people— and rightfully so—but it also tends to get results. You can use this type of system to build your own profiles in other areas of life too. For example, I've used these types of systems when playing poker and made solid choices in the game because of them.

What you want to do is start recognizing patterns and create a system that works for you that you can remember. Some people use animals—throughout this book I've used the example of predators and prey. Some people use names of people they know, and some just use their own classifications.

This is how it works: when you recognize a pattern, you're going to start seeing these patterns repeat. For example, someone who's a "social star" is cool, everyone wants to be around them. Or someone who is loud and just wants to be heard, you'll call a "loudmouth." You're going to start recognizing patterns in people that group them into certain categories.

So, there are several ways of profiling and categorizing. When you become good at it, I promise it becomes much easier and faster, and it's going to generate consistent results for you in and out of conferences and industry events.

Following are some examples of profiles that I've used. You can start with these as an example and create your own system.

The Leech => this person is the first to disappear when the bill comes to the table. They only hang around and befriend people at the event who can get them into places or pay for the table. It is <u>very transactional</u>, like a shortcut. They're short-sighted and tend to only look for what will generate money / connections or something similar for them right now.

The "Fake It 'Til You Make It" => this person will really exaggerate when it comes to their numbers. That could be the budget they manage or spend, clients they have, or just what they do. They are trying to prove themselves to others and care more about what others think of them. Their stories will always seem highly exaggerated, even when talking about a taxi taking them to a club. Everything is big and dramatic with them.

So, there are a few profiles that I use to recognize categories that certain types of people fall into and are usually pretty easy to recognize.

When you want to use this system for more than memorizing people you met at an event, you can take it to the next level, and this is based on Tony Robbins famous quote: "When people are like each other they tend to like each other." Keeping this quote in mind has allowed me to make helpful, positive predictions about people. Basically, people like people who are like them. If someone talks loudly, they are much more likely to hang around and like people who talk loudly, and they'll assume those who speak in softer tones are weak or uninteresting. Another example is distinguishing democrats from republicans because usually people who are one or the other tend to like people with the same ideals better, while staying away from the other side as much as possible.

You can use this knowledge to read into people and situations. If you know, see, hear, or recognize someone a certain way, you could adjust to a certain level. If you want to approach a loud talker, you could show that characteristic, and the chances of that person liking you have just increased.

Another example of how to use this would be knowing who to connect with. Since you know he's a republican for example, he's more likely to connect with other republicans and you can start to create your conference/mastermind entourage of people.

These are strategies for connecting with/avoiding certain people your intuition or experience tells you are people you want to attract or disengage with. You don't have to become fake or give a false representation of who you are. Just know who you'd prefer to align with, and you can present similar facets of what would draw that person to you.

THIRTEEN

CHOOSING THE RIGHT BUSINESS PARTNER

onferences are a great place to find potential partners and create new partnerships. I love this environment because you can reach a higher level of authenticity when you meet people face-to-face, rather than on Zoom calls or in standard business meetings. During a conference, it's harder for someone to mask their true self—something that is much easier to do over a Zoom or voice call. However, at a conference they can only maintain their mask for so long. It's only a matter of time until the truth, or at least parts of it, will pierce the façade. Meaning you'll see soon enough whether that person abuses drugs or tells you their true story. This will save you money and resources because you'll see that this person does not fit what you're looking for in a partner.

At the end of the day, it's all about **integrity**.

You'd be amazed (or not) to know how many people in the industry are cheating on their wives/husbands. Or they go against their beliefs, where people who wouldn't drink for religious reasons end up drinking.

It isn't difficult to identify someone you consider as having low integrity.

Just think, if that person lies to their God by not keeping their faith, or is lying to their partner in life, **who are you**, as their business partner **to them?** You're 100% next in line to get screwed over.

I am not here to preach about the holy institute of marriage, nor the importance of belief systems. What I am saying is:

1. Behavior is a good sign of how loyal a person is.
2. How a person acts can show whether they're not thinking things through clearly or if they're just completely swept up by the rush of opportunities and don't think about (or care about) the consequences.

Having said that, I've also seen very talented people who were cheaters and partied too much manage to create a lot of money. Some of them I've even been in partnerships with.

Sometimes you have to weigh the options in front of you, and while the best choice might be to wait for the right partner, a reasonable alternative could be to structure a deal where you know that you are in control of the business, regardless of the stability of that person. As long as you match your expectations to the behavior that person presents—for instance, you know this person will not be your main partner and an alliance would simply be another stage in your digital marketing career—that could be a good option. Again, as long as you are fully aware of who you're partnering with, you can manage the risks.

Another tip I'd like to offer is to be self-aware rather than naïve. I know that's hard to do, since we often don't realize when we're being naive. Typically, that's something you can only see in hindsight. But I have created some tools I've put in place to prevent myself from landing in the wrong situations.

Here are the top two considerations I use:

1. This simple method will keep you from being fooled by a lot of people. It goes like this: after each conversation or call you have with anyone, train

yourself to assume this person is lying. Now, don't get me wrong, I don't want you to really go through life thinking that everyone is a liar, this is just a system put in place to get you out of that naive state of mind and trigger that critical place in your head that we sometimes shut down when we want to trust someone or when someone is a very good salesperson. This assumption forces the brain to critique our decisions and activates the common sense we all have. *The simple fact is that sometimes I just tend to forget people lie, and I tend to assume people are truthful when they tell me things.* This system I created offers a safety net for those moments when I forget to keep my guard up, and it's helped me a lot throughout my career.

2. Be aware and listen for hints of what's to come or how they think. Everything someone says (even jokes) goes through a certain pathway inside our minds. Even a so-called joke could reveal a lot about someone's life view.

Here's a situation I've encountered:

Out of six companies and partnerships I was involved with, I had equity in two companies/partnerships—one had two partners who were just a bit older than me, and the other had three partners who were much older than me.

And while every one of my partners in the six companies knew that I recorded all my phone calls, these two sets of partners were the only ones who were concerned about the recordings. In one situation, one of the partners told me that if I don't stop recording, he'll have to end the relationship with me. In another situation, one guy was telling the other partner "Be careful, he records everything."

Back then, they actually made me feel as though I was doing something wrong. I really felt bad and tried to explain to them that I'm recording our meetings for other purposes or that I would stop recording them specifically.

Looking back this was such a huge sign of things to come with those partnerships. Turns out, they were bothered by me recording our conversations because they knew they were going to try and screw me over—and they wanted as little proof as possible of their intentions. That's why they were worried about me recording them. That should've been a major sign to tread carefully with such people.

Exclusivity Considerations

In some partnerships, potential or current partners are going to ask you to sign a contract. That contract might have some nondisclosure agreement (NDA) points within it and it also might require you to commit to either working exclusively with them or not to work in that industry or niche for a specific period of time after you are done working with them.

In my experience, I see those exclusivity expectations as predatory. This not only tells me a lot about people who ask me to sign these types of restrictive contracts, this also typically does not hold up in court because of the democratic freedom to work where you want to, depending on the country and jurisdiction.

People who ask for those types of contracts usually know that 1) they would not be able to sue you in court for it and 2) they do not have any proprietary way of operating that could really be considered a "secret."

The second part still amazes me when it happens, how much people get drunk on power when they have something going for them, and it could be as generic as content or search arbitrage, running to feeds that basically anyone could sign up to, and even though they have no technology or advantage over the competition, and their ad creatives are in the public domain. They would still act as if they invented the wheel, signing employees with NDAs and potential partners on exclusivity.

The truth is that if they really had a big, secret sauce like a SaaS product/software they developed or an impressive, exclusive contract that allows them to operate, they would not have even asked you to sign anything because they would have known that the entrance barrier to that field is too high/hard to bypass anyway.

When someone asks you to sign a noncompete contract, you should ask yourself a few things:

- Why are they trying so desperately to protect something that cannot be protected?
- Do you want to work with a partner that does not believe in prosperity?
- Is that person so inexperienced with managing partnerships and relationships that this is why he's asking you to sign this contract?

The biggest players I know who have already done a lot of deals and made a lot of money are people who believe there's enough room at the table for everyone to eat. They don't mind sharing clients, ideas, and knowledge with me or other people.

I do not suggest rejecting a deal like that just because someone asks you to sign some paperwork, but I do think you need to at least recognize the situation and address it by either:

1. Talking about this, explaining that they do not have any secret sauce, and there are enough opportunities for everyone to partake. At the end of the day, you're going to keep working together if everyone makes money and the deal is good, and not because you are committed to each other by a contract.
2. Explaining right from the start—being honest upfront that you're going to work on these types of campaigns outside of the contract/joint venture/partnership,

whether you sign it or not, because this is non-enforceable.

The main reason talking about it is important is so they recognize that you are not easily manipulated and that this is not your first rodeo.If you do not defuse this situation up front, it could have many implications later on with everything from payouts to different types of requests, especially if that person is more experienced; she might try and push the boundaries even more, and sometimes if you do not see eye to eye, it's better to let it go and move out of the deal up front than fight it later.

Weighing the Options

I'm going to tell you something that might sound like it's contradicting what I said earlier about how to choose a partner: I've also made a lot of money with people who were cheaters, didn't wake up in the morning, and were generally unstable... but I still chose them. The reason for that is that sometimes you just need what that partner has already achieved and not what they could give you in the future.

At the beginning of my career, I chose to get into the partnership with these types naively, and later on, I made that decision knowingly.

Let me explain. The concept of a partnership for most people is building a brand or business together from scratch. You do some of the work and bring some of the needed skills, and I do some of the work and bring in a different complementary skillset, right?

But what happens if that business partner already has a product or a brand, and you think that you can add to their marketing strategy? You don't really need them day to day. It's similar to acquiring a client for an agency, except that it's yours because you become a partner, so it's a partnership, but it is structured differently.

In those types of situations, consider the fact that you don't need that person active in the business, so you've lessened the risk. Life doesn't always have to be fair, and the daily work distribution might not be the fairest thing either. Alternatively, if you know that you could add value, and you go into the deal knowing that you could do it by yourself and you're not getting into a conflict with that partner over them not working or working less than you...then it might be a good idea to choose a partner with less stable/concerning qualities.

This is a classic case of being goal oriented by the way, because if your end goal is to make more money and live the life you need and want—even if you work more than the other partner and feel that it's not fair—it doesn't matter because you're still reaching your goal.

The point is to go into every situation fully aware, making sure you understand the expectations and distribution of work, and that overall, it furthers your best interests.

FOURTEEN
CHOOSING THE RIGHT AFFILIATE NETWORK OR DIRECT ADVERTISER

Now we're going to dive into some of the grittier details of digital marketing. These are important aspects to consider that are specific to this industry.

Choosing the right affiliate network or advertiser is almost like choosing your partner, isn't it? Except that they are going to be the ones who pay you, and that the relationship isn't exactly equal. On one hand, your interests are aligned—you want to drive traffic that generates as many sales as possible. But on the other hand, you are in a conflict of interest and in constant negotiation mode because you cannot be fully transparent with each other. Usually, the advertiser or network doesn't know how much you pay per conversion, and you don't know how much they are making on their end.

So, in terms of transparency and aligning interests, I would say the hierarchy is partnerships > networks > clients.

The Pros and Cons of Working with an Advertiser vs a Network:

Just like so many decisions you're going to have to make, the way you are sending traffic to an offer and who you're going to send traffic to has no one definite answer. It depends on the bankroll and payment terms you need (aka the money you can float), how many people you know and how well positioned you are with them and in general, and much more.

When considering working with one or the other, remember that working with an advertiser cuts the middleman. The network is taking a % commission of each lead or sale you generate, so it doesn't make sense to keep a middleman when you can have it all to yourself. On the other hand, some advertisers could be harder to manage, some of them may need a longer payment cycle like a month or more, or some do not pay at all. Since a network has a bigger reputation to maintain, usually it's more stable because it's running multiple offers. Even if the advertiser does not pay them, they would still pay you to keep you as an affiliate on their network. So, the interest for them is greater than any one-time advertiser. A network also can negotiate prices for you and vouch for you as an affiliate that runs a lot of traffic, and some networks can help you with lookalike audiences, creatives, and technical stuff like implementing certain pixels or setting up postbacks, where some advertisers don't have that technical support/expertise.

And by the way, I suggest you ask about that before you start running with an affiliate network or before you start scaling with them. Ask: "Are you going to pay me regardless of whether you get paid?" Believe me, the last situation you want to be in is that your affiliate manager tells you they did not get paid—and only when they get paid will you get paid. You'll have no possible way of knowing who the advertiser is or how to reach them or if the network is even telling you the truth.

As another consideration, working with an advertiser would likely get you a higher CPA, and that would allow you to scale faster, lose less money at the beginning of the campaign before you optimize, and possibly help out with creatives or landing pages that the network did not get. Yet, some networks can create those resources for you, when direct advertisers just can't fill in for the number of creatives, pre landers, and offer page optimizations you need.

The network might compensate you for losing at the beginning just to keep your campaign running, and some advertisers would also give you a testing budget so that you won't lose money at the beginning.

To summarize, I don't think there's a specific answer, but there are a couple of rules, or spectrum because the right approach can be specific to each deal:

- If you do not like or you're just not good at keeping relationships.
- If the offer has a higher margin.
- If you don't have a lot of cash flow or are afraid you are not going to get paid.
- If the offer is scaling and you need more buyers for the traffic (like for example if you're selling leads and generating more than the maximum a buyer could buy).

Those, or each one on its own, should be a good reason for you to work with a network.

When you work with a direct advertiser, usually there's a bit more risk and a bit more to manage with far more rewards when it works.

It all comes down to three things 1) knowing what you need, 2) knowing what your weaknesses are, 3) direct communication —talking about it with the advertiser or the network. If you know that your weakness is cash flow or creatives, ask them if they'll be able to provide that for you, and then make the best decision for you. It's not like amateurs are running only with direct advertisers, and it's not like they're only running with networks. It's all about the specific situation and particular offer.

· · ·

Finding Direct Advertisers and Networks

While networks usually do some advertising, promote themselves, and present in booths at conferences, direct advertisers are harder to come across. Having said that, it's still possible.

One of the easiest ways would be leaving your phone number on the landing page if it's a lead generation campaign. Or you could contact customer support on the offer you see and ask to talk to someone who's in charge of advertising.

Beyond those two options, I'd highly recommend going with the more veteran networks out there while keeping in mind that the newer ones might be more competitive and eager to prove themselves. Again, it's a high-risk, high-reward situation because the newer networks have a greater likelihood of not paying you or having other problems you'll have to face.

I was consulting someone recently who told me he doesn't want to run with a certain network because everyone knows about them and to him, they seem too generic. I told him that I know of many people who are making money with them. The mentality of looking for something exclusive that no one else has isn't always the best way to go when considering whom you're going to work for. Remember that at the end of the day, we're all buying ads, and people can see everyone's ads, because that's the nature of ads. If something is out there, well, it's out there for all to see.

Launching Traffic to Direct Advertisers and Networks

While a network usually has a streamlined affiliate onboarding process, some advertisers might not have the right technology or even know-how to support you, and you need to keep that in mind. If you trust that advertiser and you have somewhat of a right attribution and you establish a very specific way of measuring your conversions, and that is clear and agreed upon, you both should be good.

When compared to the direct advertiser relationship where

you really need—or at least should have—good communication with the person you work with, partnering with a network saves you that time or effort. This is because the network acts as a bridge to the advertiser. If the network mentions a specific affiliate, you have leverage even before you launched the campaign and sent a few clicks to them.

Understanding that a network not only saves time and effort in managing the advertiser, but also contributes to a long-term relationship is crucial. For example, if you've previously worked with that network and they know you can scale campaigns profitably, their recommendation to the end advertiser can help you with payouts or payment terms right out of the gate. In contrast, establishing that level of trust and rapport with a direct advertiser might take you more time.

Dealing with direct advertisers might take longer as they would want to test and see where your traffic is coming from, or the lead quality, or the AOV you can provide them. It will take more time to build rapport, on both sides.

FIFTEEN
FINDING WHAT'S WORKING RIGHT NOW

That's the million-dollar question...what's working right now?

There are so many ways of figuring this out, and this topic also really overlaps with what we talked about at the beginning of this book regarding how you start, because a big part of how to start is figuring out what's working right now.

But the first question you need to ask yourself is: Do you want to build something of your own? A big creative project? Or are you into whatever's working? And that goes back to the unfair advantage concept we talked about earlier in this book.

Most of you are probably looking for whatever's working right now. You're looking for a stream of cash flow to begin with, and grow from there, and that's okay. That approach, honestly, could also be a good way of finding out what you want to develop for yourself later on as a brand owner by taking whatever's working and improving upon it.

There are a few ways on doing that research:

1. Conferences
2. Facebook groups
3. Forums like STM

4. Looking at whatever's running - spy tools or just Instagram/Facebook/YouTube users with VPN

The Myth of Focusing on One Specific Thing

One of the hardest currents you have to swim against, that took me time to overcome, was that common internal dialogue that says *things are not going to work out for me*. Or thinking that if you do not focus on one specific thing, you'll fail. That kind of thinking is a recipe for disaster.

For me it took time and going on a minor spiritual journey to understand that not all people are built the same or think the same. One thing that works for you, like focusing on one specific project and company, could be what's going to kill the spirit of someone who likes to move fast, learn fast, and gets tired of the "same old thing" fast.

It took time to learn that I like to move around, that I get frustrated when things are moving slowly. It took time to understand that it's okay that I change my mind a lot and that I almost completely change my career every five years...even if everyone else is thinking that I've lost my way.

What I'm trying to say is that if you are (and you probably are) listening and watching those Instagram reels and TikTok videos where so many people are talking about how to do things with confidence, it might make you feel unstable and cause you to think that you are not going down the right path. Understand that these people are telling you 80% of what they've heard and what they believe is true and 20% of what's worked for them. Their opinion does not mean anything regarding **your** journey and **your** path. You need to listen to yourself, find whatever's moving and whatever's stopping you by researching your past and diving deep into it when you find that path.

Just like any entrepreneur and affiliate or agency owner, you're going to have times where everything seems to fail, when your campaigns or client's campaigns are going to lose money. Times when you're going to have difficulty recruiting clients and finding new offers to run, when you might be asked to pause current offers that are making money and even lose clients on the way.

During a dry season, I had to deal with the same issues... more than once.

I remember talking with a friend and telling him that everything was so hard, and complaining about the situation I was in. He told me something that was and will always be true: "The money is out there, people are making money, it just changes direction."

Money-making never stops—it's just about finding out where it is.

There are two methods that almost always work for me:

Method 1:

Looking at whatever's running right now, this could be accomplished with third party tools, using tools that are available for everyone like the Facebook ads library, or just scrolling through your own feed if you're searching for whatever's running in your country.

Some people don't make the separation between whatever's **running** and whatever's **WORKING** - keep in mind the fact that it's running means one of two things:

1. The market might be more saturated in that specific niche.
2. The campaigns are not working, and people keep spending money on them—sometimes because they believe they will eventually make it work, sometimes because they don't understand they are losing money, and sometimes just because they have large sums of their client's money, and they are spending all of it. That client doesn't understand the metrics well enough to realize he's losing money.

So again, the fact that you see a campaign running can ONLY be used as inspiration. It does not mean that it's profitable or that the person running it is even aiming towards profitability. Sometimes they will acquire customers and build it towards an exit, for example, and other times they will be profitable, but the profit is made on the back end, selling other things you do not see beyond that front-end product you do see.

The more zoomed-out version of this, outside of digital marketing, would be looking for where the money is going in general, looking for trends. This could be done in so many ways, from understanding the economy better to using tools like Google trends.

Method 2:

Going to conferences, knowing the bigger publishers or networks, going to their booths to see who they meet with, and talking to them. This method is very old school, and it could be a sharp tool in the right hands of someone who's good at networking and has made a lot of money.

There are so many good things about this method—you don't pay money/commissions for the intro, you're able to spy and get a lot of information quickly, and you can really level up your game and partnerships in one conference. The only thing you need to remember is having a networking-memory system in place, meaning you're going to meet a lot of people and you must have a system to remember everyone and make sure you follow up after the conference.

Different Types of Offers

There are so many angles through which to look at offers and try to find what's working and what you're going to approach next.

Another way of finding what you're going to run is by looking at the ever-green niches like weight loss or insurance and starting from there. (While the first option I suggested was really the opposite, try looking at whatever's right now running "on the ground".)

When your research is niche specific, it is my experience that you're going to find different results.

Yet another way to look at things is through the scope of low and high barrier entry levels. In general, the higher barrier industries, projects, and niches are going to require more networking, more money and sometimes just more patience, they are built for someone who's already making money and looking to expand. The lower barrier industries will be easier to get into but will likely be more saturated and more difficult for you to protect or gain any advantage.

It's up to you to know yourself 1) technically when it comes to your skill set and money and 2) spiritually or mentally when it comes to having the guts to play a bigger game that requires patience.

For example, running an insurance offer might be easier than creating a supplement brand. Creating that supplement brand might be easier than creating a payment processing platform. Creating a processing platform might be easier than building a casino platform and getting the permits, and so on.

SIXTEEN
TESTING THE INITIAL OFFER/RELATIONSHIP:

Over the years, I've had people offer me certain deals that didn't make mathematical sense. For example, when I asked them what CPA they were getting on that same offer they told me $40 and offered it to me at $35.

That, of course, doesn't make sense... The likelihood of me being able to bring sales for less than whatever they are buying after optimizing is low. Even if I would have been able to do it, then it's still non-scalable, so they are either looking for a different type of traffic (like email for example), or they do not know enough about how affiliate marketing or media buying works. Or sometimes they just want to take advantage of affiliate traffic.

In those types of situations, I like to test the relationship or deal and see how much they believe this could work. I make one of the following requests:

- Work on an agency model, where I get a % of ad spend or profit share.
- Have them pay for the initial $5-10k, as a testing budget and then move to a CPA deal.

- Create a deal that's based on a small amount of money being paid for each sale, while they pay for the media.

Anyone who believes the CPA they provided is sustainable and that his offer really converts should feel secure enough to want to continue with one of these options.

This should be a good test for any type of deal—don't forget you have the power. The person who holds the traffic, the affiliate in that case, would always be in charge, unless that offer is truly amazing and then we're back to the usual supply and demand rules.

Managing the Relationship

I've had situations where I had a very specific deal with an exclusive offer. It was an agency model deal where I wasn't risking my own money and we ran traffic at high volume and generated over $5 million revenue in a month.

I worked with a few other people on that deal who were in charge of copywriting, building funnels, and sending out emails and SMS texts.

One day the owner of the company decided to change the deal, but he didn't update anyone. He didn't mention that change to anyone, and I ended up seeing a number that's 30% less than what I expected in my bank account at the end of the month.

Those other people who worked with me on this project didn't feel we had enough leverage inside the deal to even consider it. They just decided to accept it because even when we're talking about 30% less, it was still a very good deal that generated significant money.

I explained to them how weak that move that was. What does it say about us as a team or as individual professionals if we just accept whatever that person decides for us, if we let him change the deal without even updating us about it?

We weren't employed by him; we were offering our services to him. We set our prices and he could decide if he wanted to hire us or not. We are like a high-end store, not a marketplace where you can negotiate prices.

What does that say about how much we believe we are worth? When you go and buy a Mercedes or a Bentley, they don't tell you, "Just give us whatever you believe that car is worth, and we'll just take it and shut up." No, they have specific pricing. And you decide as a client whether you can pay or if you want it at that price.

Here, the client gets a tailor-made Italian car, meaning us as a team. And the way I saw it, there was no reason for us to shut up about it and just accept whatever he's giving us.

Positioning is so important, not just for negotiation's sake, but also for how you feel inside the relationship in your day-to-day life.

The client always needs to know you are not dependent on them and are willing to leave at any point. I believe the same about relationships beyond business.

A strategy that could help you get there in terms of positioning yourself better in front of a client could be what I call "planting the seed." When in a call with someone, they need to know one of two things about you:

1. You always have other options. You're usually just capping your own number of clients or offers that you're running because you want to stay focused, but finding another big client or good offer is easy. You've done it a hundred times.
2. You're not really that satisfied with the current payout you're getting—it's barely enough for you. This is more advanced and could be risky, as you do not want to be at a place where the other side feels unstable in the relationship. So every time you let them know you deserve more, you should always

stabilize it by saying that you believe in the company or brand long term.

In the next chapter, we'll talk about how to stabilize the deal.

SEVENTEEN
STABILIZING THE DEAL

O kay, so you've started running with an advertiser or a network—perfect. You probably got the "street" CPA, an initial CPA to see if you're worth spending time on.

There's almost always going to be a call in the first month or two of you running that offer where you set the first round of numbers, talk about benchmark conversion rates (if this is a lead campaign), and set the right economics of the deal.

This happens with agency clients and with affiliate offers. It could come from you initiating it or the client, but if you're running high volume the call would take place in the first week or two.

Everyone's checking in their numbers. If it's an ecom/VSL campaign, the advertiser wants to know that there are no chargebacks and that the AOV (and possibly later on the LTV) is where he needs it to be. Or if it's a lead-gen campaign, the advertiser wants to know that the leads are in line with his benchmark and that they are converting to sales at the end. Meanwhile, you're checking your conversion rates, confirming that you're profitable, and optimizing landing pages and creatives.

· · ·

What to Watch for in These Calls:

Look out for anything that does not make sense—always ask yourself during the call, after the call, and later when going through the call (I always like to record those calls and go through them later), "Does this make sense?" If it doesn't, you need to start asking questions.

Let me give you an example. I worked with a big affiliate network that had an internal offer: lead generation for a certain industry. I'd been running it for a month, and I'd just started breaking even or making a profit.

We went on a call they requested, and they started to ask me if I'm currently making money on my end, because the economics have to work out and they have a very small conversion rate that's much lower than what they're used to; they are used to having 10%–15% of leads convert, and they're getting 5% with my traffic.

They went on to say that the client they are selling the leads to is the one driving the car here and that he makes the decisions about this offer.

We talked about how to potentially get the conversion rate higher and optimize…and then they revealed that this specific client **really doesn't want to share information** about their conversion rates and that we might need to lower the CPL that they're paying me later on in order to stabilize the lower conversion rates.

We closed the call, and I started thinking about what they said. Two red flags immediately went up:

1. The fact that they were trying to say from the beginning that if they would have to drop the CPL that they are paying me, it's not going to be on their end, it's because this comes from the client's side. I did not believe that because they already told me they were making money on their end so that didn't make sense.

2. The fact that it doesn't make any sense that they are talking about conversion rates being low on one hand and that on the other hand, they are also saying that this client doesn't share his conversion rates with them, so how can they know if it's 5% or 10%? The only way they would know what the conversion rates are (to purchase) is by getting that information from their client, and if he doesn't share the information... how could they know it's low, or that it's any specific number?

That's why I want to share with you a solid strategy for those situations—and in any negotiation—with a client and as an affiliate.

A "**blocking bet**" is a good move that stabilizes payouts/deals, even temporarily, and gives you back control: making a request for higher CPA or CPL when you know that a potential payout drop is coming or when you think the advertiser might shave you.

A blocking bet comes from the world of poker terminology— you think that that person is going to raise you a substantial amount or you know that he's leading the action on a hand you're playing right now and you can make a move before they do. **You raise them a lower amount so that they either pay you that amount or, even if they raise you, it's not as high as they initially would have.**

This causes a situation where you essentially take control over the hand, because most people would just pay what you raised and some people might raise anyway, but still taking a few steps back, you win anyway.

The reason this is a strong move is because in negotiation, saying the first number, aka "anchoring," is creating a situation where the negotiation starts from the number you say, and most people do not know how to defuse those situations.

For example, if I know that you have a strong hand (or, going back to business terminology, that you have leverage over me) in that deal and you're going to request something, that changes the deal for the worse on my side. That could mean a paycheck cut, salary cut, lowering payouts on an affiliate deal, adding more filters on what type of traffic I can buy, or what creatives I could use or capping the volume of leads you can send.

Knowing this is coming, the best moves are to defuse the situation by blocking it by saying that I don't make enough money on that offer, OR by requesting a raise. When you make the first move, you "anchor" the conversation in your favor and the other side needs to respond to that. All of the sudden, a salary cut looks a lot farther away and maybe he will just want to keep your salary or payout as is to keep you going.

In the last conversation example above, we are talking about a classic scenario for a blocking bet. Why? Because they already told me that "in the near future" they would like to make a change—either make the lead form harder, which is going to result in a higher CPL for me, or drop the payout, because the conversion rates "are not there."

What I did was I went on a call with them and told them that some days I'm losing money (wasn't a lie) and some I'm making money, but I wanted them to start considering raising the payout so that the campaign would stabilize on my end and also would be scalable—a classic blocking bet move. And it worked because at the very least they wanted to maintain the CPL for a long time after that request.

So, I recognized it was coming because they went and told me that that's what they were planning—a weak/amateur move on their part. I planned ahead and attacked with a faster response that they could not defuse. We ended up running at the same CPL for a while and even raised it a bit later on.

I want to give you two more examples, from real-life experiences that happened to me, to better explain how to recognize and better react to similar experiences.

Real-Life Example 1

I was running a lead gen campaign for an affiliate network that claimed they were giving me 100% rev share, saying that they made money only on the back-end of the offer, meaning the upsells, using the data like emails and SMS to monetize that traffic later, but mainly from the "thank you page" that came after the lead was submitted by the user.

When I asked them if I could use my own landing pages to optimize for leads and send them the info through API—also known as "hosting and posting" (H&P)—they asked their manager who then said that it might be an option.

I immediately understood that they were lying about the 100% revenue share, because if someone's business model is dependent on the backend revenue, why would he let me post the lead info if that causes him to lose the "thank you" page where he said he's making all his money? All they would have left are the emails and SMS, and yes, they could be making a lot of money on that data, but they specifically said that most of it comes from the "thank you" page.

That allowed me to first understand my positioning in the deal, and second to know when and how they look when they are lying to me. Most importantly, I understood that I could ask for more and push better terms that I wouldn't push if I didn't feel comfortable with where I stood.

Real-Life Example 2

On another lead gen campaign, I asked what was the highest CPL I'd be able to get if my lead quality was good. The network's affiliate manager was really not into answering that question directly. She started talking about EPC and how that's all that matters. While she is absolutely right and it really does come down to EPC, she said that they are optimizing each and every affiliate's traffic on their backend and making changes to the funnel.

I didn't believe her because if 20 affiliates send traffic through Facebook, then the page must already be optimized as they are getting the same type of traffic at the end of the day and there would be a level to how much they could have optimized that page.

I went ahead and checked after a while to see if the funnel changed in any way...it had not altered. Then I got on a call with her and asked her to never bullshit me again because I am looking for an honest business relationship and transparent communication.

EIGHTEEN
GETTING INTO THE
ECONOMICS OF THE DEAL

n order to make a decision on pricing within a negotiation, you have to understand the economics of the other side.

Here's a list of things to check or ask yourself, the current advertiser, and other advertisers in the industry when you decide that you have a solid niche and campaign working for you and you want to figure out **how to scale**:

A. Payout/Cash Questions:

- What are the industry payout benchmarks?
- What are other affiliate networks paying for the same offer/s?
- What are the "street" payouts and how high can they go?
- What's the usual rejection/acceptance rate on those leads?

B. Can I get some direct advertisers, and how much can they pay me?

- Sometimes a simple LinkedIn or Google search will lead you to some direct advertisers to work with.

C. The advertiser and offer stats:

- What are the numbers on the advertiser and network side?
- What's their AOV? LTV?
- Is there a subscription?
- What are their conversion rates from lead to a client?
- Are they using their own system or a system they control to show you how much you made?

D. When you get deeper into the industry:

- At some point you're also going to have friends you can trust who might be running the same type of offer, and you could ask them how they run, their earnings per click (EPCs)...this could put you far ahead.

Negotiating any deal without those numbers or specific information is like trying to operate in a dark room. You're going to hit a wall at some point, and even worse, sometimes you're not going to know it, meaning you could potentially stubbornly request things that really cannot happen because they are so far off the benchmarks and the numbers.

Using common sense is also key. For example, you know that on Facebook, running lead-gen campaigns, CPC is going to be $2-$5, because it depends on the creatives, the time of year and the niche, but let's say you've run that specific type of offer and you know specifics about the CPCs, you know that the lead disqualification rate (the % of leads you are actually getting paid on) is 10%, which means that even with a 10% conversion rate to lead (that's a lot), we're talking about a price per lead of $20-$50. Since we have a rejection rate of 90%, we have to multiply this by 10, meaning an actual paid lead would cost us around $200-$500.

Even if our numbers are really off, and conversion rate is

double that, or CPCs are half that, we still should be looking at those numbers and comparing them to the payout. So if the payout is $50 per qualified lead, we shouldn't even try to run this campaign, as numbers do not make any sense. This will tell you, usually, that the traffic the advertiser is looking for is email traffic (or worse, that the advertiser doesn't know his own numbers).

This is why **working with an advertiser or network that knows their numbers is crucial** so you're not losing time or money on campaigns that just won't work. The math never lies.

Use Analogies in Negotiations

Using *analogies* in a negotiation is something I really like because it generates excellent results for me.

I believe some of it has to do with the fact that it allows you to step out of the conversation, lets egos take a break, and you don't have to use any examples that refer to the other person's real life. When you give a specific example that has to do with someone or someone's business, they will likely become defensive. That's why this tool is so powerful...it allows you to express your point without making it personal.

For example, if you talk to someone who's telling you they are trying a certain thing, and they keep buying the cheapest solution that holds up for a short time for them, talking about how buying the cheapest solution might sound like too much of a criticism and could create the opposite impact of what you want. Instead, you could give a car analogy and talk about how investing in a more expensive car might be a better solution for the long term. This is a safe, relatable example that allows you both to step out of the situation and understand with less ego involved.

When you combine understanding people with understanding the economics of the deal, you'll gain confidence when negotiating low stakes deals while growing your self-confidence.

This could be an amazing tool to generate positive results in any negotiation.

At the end of the day, remember that if they control the "admin" platform and system that shows you the sales and payout, they can change the numbers easily, so your CPA/CPL or rev-share really doesn't matter. The best way to transfer some of the power back to you is letting them know that you're a/b testing your traffic with other places, and you're optimizing according to EPC. If they lose, you're going to allocate all the traffic to the winner. That's going to keep them on their toes, and even though you won't have transparency into their numbers and system, you'll still have the chance to negotiate better and make more money.

NINETEEN
PRICING IT RIGHT

I f you ask most veteran agency owners, they'll tell you that the pricing game has one main catch: maximizing LTV (lifetime value of a client)—the total amount of time the client stays with you and the amount of money you make from them throughout the longest time period.

AOV * LTV = $$$

Monthly payment * number of months = what you generate from that client.

Where this gets complicated is when we talk about the balance needed between the amount the client pays monthly (monthly retainer/AOV) and the number of months that client stays. Usually, clients that pay less will stick around longer, and clients that spend more go looking for ways to save money and stay for shorter periods of time.

As the agency, you typically want to work on a deal where you get the upside, meaning creating a hybrid deal where when the client makes money, you make money—and that's where it gets tricky. Often, at the beginning, the client wants you to have that incentive and generate more money for him, but when you do, and you invoice them a larger amount of money, they start thinking of how they could save that money.

Usually what happens with clients that scale and have a revenue/profit share deal with the agency is that when they start to pay $20k-$30k-$40k a month, they try to cut you out to save that money. This is an absurd way of thinking since they paid you to get a job done, you did it, and you probably even exceeded their expectations. And now they're going to fire you/switch you for another agency. Unfortunately, that's the way it works. When the campaign loses, it's your fault, yet when the campaign is making money, it's because of their product or decisions.

One of the keys to solving this issue, and finding that specific balance in a deal, is understanding the person who actually makes the calls inside the company. Is she a person who enjoys giving and wants stability? Does she understand that she might pay a lot and that it's a good sign that she's paying more?

I've had clients tell me that they enjoy writing the biggest wires to me…and they love increasing it because that means that they are making more money. I've also had clients that were just optimizing all the time, including trying to get an internal media buying team to replace me.

The total impact you can have on these scenarios is honestly low. The more time you spend in this industry, you learn to expect and predict this, and you also learn to read people and what they want when their campaigns start making money. The small opportunities in this area would include options like introducing them to an idea that the more money you make them, the more they pay you so that they are prepared and not surprised when that happens. Or you could also cap the maximum you make from the deal so that both of you are in a comfortable space.

Another option for greater impact is creating and giving more value. If all you do is media buying, then that client could replace you easily. But if you also have a specific system/platform that helps them see more value such as analytics—or if you offer the creatives for them, that could be added value to make it harder for them to replace you, internally or externally.

TWENTY
DEALING WITH CHANGE

Throughout the business relationship, especially when it's a new relationship and particularly with lead-gen campaigns, **changes will happen**. The advertiser will likely optimize on their end, and they might ask you to either add or change content on the lead form or landing page, or they might ask you to target only specific ages or states. Some will even become aggressive and tell you they will not pay for more traffic now or try to limit the types of platforms you can buy on, for example.

I've seen affiliates go on a rampage when that happens, pushing the advertiser and throwing out ultimatums. This never works as it doesn't hold up. Even if you convince the advertiser to keep the deal as it is, he's still not going to be satisfied, and you're likely to repeat that conversation again several more times in the near future.

The best way to deal with this is to understand why he needs to make those changes, and if it makes sense. Is it possible he's been misled by his agency or someone with a different interest than yours regarding your campaign? Sometimes you'll be able to come up with a different solution that addresses the reason he gave for making those changes. Even if your solution doesn't immediately solve the issue, you'll get more clarity on your traffic or where the offer currently stands in terms of optimization. Then you'll have a better idea of how to improve your traffic. For example, he'll tell you that he doesn't like the age of the leads you are sending right now, and you could make changes other than limiting the age.

My experience in dealing with those kinds of requests include:

1. Explaining that not everything could be put into the campaign, meaning not everything has to do with the campaign/platform or is the affiliate's responsibility. *For example*, advertisers often want to change the deal because of high refund rates, low conversion rates, or just higher conversion rates in some age groups or states. You need to explain to them that not everything has to do with the campaign and your side. Some things fall under their responsibility like merchant accounts, sales pitch, pricing and product/services quality, their email and SMS marketing on the backend, the copy (text quality) that they are using, or even their reputation/authority as a brand.

2. Explaining to them that every time you make a change to the campaign, the campaign (regardless of the platform) will go back into learning mode again, meaning it resets and starts to learn who the campaign's audience is, as if you just launched that campaign from scratch. And that costs you money, because up to now, the campaign is stabilized on a decent CPA. Remember: It's okay to make changes, as long as it's not too frequent, unless that also affects the payout CPA you're getting. Also, when making changes, don't make them "sharp," but instead, fade them in while the old ads/campaigns fade out.

3. Explaining to them that, ultimately, it's all about economics. It's okay if they ask you to add 20 more fields to the form. It's okay if they ask you to remove any language that might be problematic during the sale or later during customer service, but that needs to be calculated and priced into the payout you're getting. These requests will change the metrics within your campaign, so simply explain how CPC x CVR (conversion rate) results in your CPA, and that every field you add to the form will cause a lower CVR, resulting in a higher CPA. That usually does the trick.

Advertisers will want to optimize according to whatever is working for them. I've had advertisers tell me that a specific campaign works really well for them in specific states. I gave those states a go and saw that the CPA was twice as much as other places I was targeting, or when I'm targeting very broadly. So again, it's okay if those leads or sales are better for them in a specific state, but that also has to reflect on the payout they are giving me.

I have also had advertisers ask me to add ridiculous "overkill" fields to the lead landing page. I explained these are items that should be part of the sales script and requested over the phone—there's no reason to make the landing page more complicated for the user.

I'm always trying to remind myself that some advertisers have great products, companies, and services, but they might not understand digital marketing and how it works. And that's okay, that's the reason they need you, the reason you need them, and the reason you're making money from them.

It's hard to find an advertiser or a network that has smart people *and* understands their own business—who have the guts to play a big game and also understand digital marketing. What *you* must understand is this is all part of the game *you'll* have to play... just like understanding the media buying and dealing with platforms.

The types of situations I've described in this chapter are inevitable. They will happen at some point. Instead of fighting them, create an opportunity from them and make lemonade out of lemons.

These could also be great opportunities to ask for a payout bump if you believe there's room for it. Or at least teach the advertiser that when they ask for things, you can ask for things too. Then they might think twice before requesting you to add some new fields to the landing page or remove language that helps you sell.

Remember "blocking bets" I mentioned earlier? The situations mentioned in this chapter illustrate the times to use them if you see that an advertiser is asking for too many changes.

TWENTY-ONE
SHORT-TERM
PLAY/LONG-TERM PLAY

I n business I've met people with different strategies when it comes to running our joint venture or their businesses. Some could not stick to one business or strategy and lost focus. Sometimes it didn't make money right away and they were so married to a project or business that they lost money while they continued believing it would turn profitable someday. You can apply short-term or long-term play methodologies when looking at the micro-level regarding campaigns.

Examples of a Long-Term Play:

1. Having the ability to lose some money at the beginning in order to optimize, build relationships, and have a greater leverage when asking for a payout bump.
2. Running a campaign on a low margin to get into an exclusive pool of offers.
3. Losing on one campaign to make money on the other one.

4. Targeting quality over quantity; if we're talking about the economics game, then we want higher LTVs; if we're talking about the lead-gen game, higher conversion rates.

5. Investing the money you're making from the first profitable platform into new platforms so that the campaign would be more stable and scalable down the road.

The long-term play is great when you believe the advertiser is making enough margin on their end. I personally suggest **using the long-term play only with trusted advertisers and products that are sustainable** for at least a year from when you start, i.e., nothing trendy like soap during the COVID pandemic or A/C during the summertime.

Cons: you need deep pockets, guts, and the ability to endure losing money in order to build the relationship, show that you are a team player, and create leverage.

Pros: you create unparalleled leverage in the deal, holding the advantage over the advertiser.

Get a lot of data and be able to optimize. The campaigns are going to be a lot more stable because you haven't pushed them to the point where you'll just need to build them up again every five days. This data also means they are easier to scale on platforms like Google Ads because you can make more decisions.

Examples of a Short-Term Play:

1. You don't see the relationship with that advertiser or affiliate network as a serious relationship.

2. You're not sure if you're going to get paid on time—or at all, if that partner shows lack of stability when and unstable payments.

3. Campaigns are seasonal or trendy—it's only a matter of time till the market will get saturated with copycats, policy is going to change, or weather is going to change; for example, masks during COVID/political merchandise/air conditioning.
4. The advertiser looks unstable in terms of daily/monthly caps or does not know how to measure, lacking attribution and cash flow.
5. The advertiser looks like he's more into learning what you do, copying it, and cutting you off...or you do not see yourself in this relationship in the future.
6. The advertiser will not share the real numbers on his side or not share numbers at all.

We might consider a short-term approach where we optimize more aggressively, shoot for the quick money, and ask for bigger payouts faster when we get some sort of leverage. Also try to be more reliant on remarketing and MOF (middle of funnel) traffic if possible.

When advertisers are into the short-term game, you have to adjust to the short-term game too; either because of the nature of the product or because of the way you see them act in the business relationship. For example, an advertiser that has a history of just "looking for the secret sauce," you know he just wants to see what's working, copy it into his internal campaigns, and cut you off. These advertisers forget that this method is completely useless in the long run, because the techniques are so dynamic and constantly changing, whatever they learned might help them for a while, but it's not going to last for long. They burn themselves by moving on.

Key Takeaways for Short-term Products or Advertisers:

1. Always make sure that you get paid weekly.
2. Know the numbers on the other side, or at least try to so you can make adjustments on your end as to how aggressive you want to be.
3. Know when to **put a limit** on how aggressive you want to be. Don't forget, the industry isn't that big. People will talk about you if you push it too far, or overpromising what doesn't exist on the creative or landing page, pushing garbage incentive traffic or any traffic that was not pre-approved by the advertiser, re-selling the leads or running on branded traffic when not approved—these tactics will put you in risky place, and I do not suggest you do that, even as a short-term play.

Bottom line is, know the difference and balance between short-term partnership and being aggressive to make sure you keep your own name clean.

Also, another tip would be generally staying away from short-term ideas, unless:

1. ROI is huge or the campaign is super easy right now.
2. That advertiser is switching offers every time one goes down, so they are trendy, but the relationship isn't fluctuating as easily.
3. You've been dragged into one, thinking that it's not a short-term deal but then you discovered it is and you're already invested in that campaign that's generating money for you (or you're looking to get back some of that money you lost/invested on it).

There are actually a few studies I've found that, in business in general, looking for and acting on the "white hat" approach will end up making more money for you than any short-term deal.

So, unless you really want that specific deal, the smarter move I've learned to take is just move away from those types of deals. Usually the best opportunities, relationships, and business take time—and there's little you can do to speed up the process.

Asking for a Payout Bump:

No one, especially not seasoned players, likes feeling extorted or pushed around.

Learning how to ask for a raise, even if you work for someone, is really important.

You always want to start and maintain a good, positive vibe throughout these kinds of conversations.

One way of doing that can be what I call the "sandwich method" that consists of a positive beginning, where you talk about how good the offer is and how nice it is working with the other person and how amazing the relationship is, or the future you see for both of you together. Then you follow this with a complaint, a problem or something that needs to be changed and why you're asking for this change. Finally, you follow up with a positive ending that talks about the future, how great this relationship could be, and how much money or positive change this discussion can mean for both sides.

For example:

1. Going on a call saying that you want to expand the relationship and business with them, that you have more bandwidth, and you want to take on more work and volume—because you love the relationship, you want to grow with them.
2. Explaining that current payout would not allow for scale because every time you raise budgets you are getting crushed and that the only way to really scale would be getting the payout up, you could also use

math to explain why current payout is unsustainable with current conversion rates and current CPCs.

3. Explaining that theoretically, in the ideas you presented, traffic could grow by 50%, and the campaigns would be much more stable, which might also allow you to run this campaign on more networks and platforms.

Here are some further ideas and strategies that could work. Some might be a bit more aggressive, and some might require you to lose some money at the beginning. The idea is to use these for inspiration and not copy/paste them into your real-life discussions:

1. Starting that campaign/running the offer regardless of payout, creating a good number of good quality leads/sales, even if you have to lose money and when the advertiser depends on it and sees that you are serious, you'll have much more leverage when asking for a payout bump. This should only be used when you either really believe in a long-term relationship with the offer owner/advertiser or when you really believe that they could pay more—and they would rather do that instead of losing you as a publisher. Also, at the end of the day, advertisers and networks look at you differently when you're currently running something and generating them cash. You would do the same if the situation was reversed.

2. Auctioning between networks and advertisers, letting the other one know that you're always a/b testing and sending at least 50% of traffic to another offer that's doing better, and what he should do in order to get **all** of your traffic. In general, letting them know that you're not sending all the traffic to them is a smart move (even if you

are) because they believe that you have a way of testing them and measuring them against a benchmark. They'll understand that their margin doesn't really matter to you, what matters is if they are outperforming the other offer. This is good when it's a wide-range, non-branded offer, like life insurance, health insurance, loans, etc.

TWENTY-TWO
KEEPING IT DYNAMIC –
DIVERSIFYING IS KEY

've seen it happen to other people, and it also happened to me over and over…you either focus on one ad platform you buy ads on, or you depend on one place/platform too much —a platform like Amazon for example. A huge part of the industry is highly dependent on this site, and sometimes they will have a year or two where they will absolutely dominate their space, and then…something happens. Amazon decides to put a product like theirs on the website for a cheaper price or it changes the ranking algorithm. Maybe Facebook changes their policy, and you have to readjust your approach to them as an ad platform.

This strategy is very good if you catch the wave early, and if you're up for a **short-term** money solution, even if this could last for a year or more.

This is **not** what I would recommend for making money in the **long-term** or creating any kind of stability. This has been researched by many in the industry, and they keep coming back with the same answer: white hat, solid, long-term strategies, always make more money and will always affect your lifestyle for the better.

Any situation where you "go all in on one hand," is

dangerous and unstable, but you didn't buy this book to hear the same stuff that's on every Instagram or TikTok reel. The biggest thing I don't hear enough people talk about is that *it doesn't feel like you're betting everything on one hand at the time you're doing it.*

When you are mostly dependent on Facebook, for example, you'll tell yourself that you have a lot of clients or that it's different niches—but really, you're just lying to yourself because you know that the only source or main source of revenue is dependent on Facebook in that example. When Facebook falls or changes course, you're going down with it, and you will have nothing else left.

Just look at the number of people you've seen make a small amount of money throughout the years, while they were building their brand, company, or product and then they exited for a huge amount of money.

This goes for anyone who has been a pioneer in his field but also for people who decided to build something that would probably only make money in the long run. Mr. Beast's YouTube channel is a perfect example of that. The guy believed in YouTube from the time he started even though everyone thought he was crazy. He dropped out of school and went all-in on being a YouTuber because he understood this would be a good future for him. He didn't make money from that, and it took him many years to perfect what he does right now. Maybe there were people who did it better, were smarter, or had more money, but those others all gave up after a few years. Mr. Beast won in the end. Consistency and obsession win overall.

At the end of the day, there can be two very different approaches. One is focused on doing what you're good at, and the other suggests you create stabilization by opening and touching as much stuff as you can.

It is my belief, in the end, success is about both risk management as well as finding the right middle ground for you, meaning you learn how deep you want to focus on one project and remembering that 20% of your work and time would generate 80% of the money, and this would happen in any project you open up.

Personally, I think that focusing on one avenue isn't a smart move, unless it also diversifies within and is not dependent on one major source of income. For example, if you have an arbitrage operation, and you sell ads on your website to five different places, that's okay, but if your business is 90% dependent on Google's AdSense, then I would not recommend this.

Another example would be if you're into lead generation and generating leads for both yourself and three other places. It would be a good idea that could help create that diversification, as long as you're not mainly buying media on Facebook or TikTok and separating it/dividing the traffic between these platforms.

I want to add that focusing on several avenues might not be the right fit for you. You really have to know yourself before you get started. It took me years to understand that I'm the type of guy that works better when I have a lot on my plate. Others who have a lot to focus on get anxiety. So, make sure you know what type of person you are before making that decision or just go with what's making you feel that "hell yeah" level of excitement.

When you have a long-term strategy, it's okay to have milestones or stops along the way that are dependent on shorter term strategies, as long as you don't get sucked into the short-term thing.

My dad always said, "Nothing is more permanent than a temporary solution." That's true, so when you're inside the daily grind, you need to make sure you ask yourself every once in a while if you're following up with the bigger, long-term strategy.

Here's an example for planning your short-to-long term strategy: you might own an agency that's highly dependent on Facebook, so your plan would be to reach a certain amount of revenue or % of profit goal with every client and then move them into another platform (such as Google) and scale there.

Another example could be setting up an agency and deciding

that when you reach a certain amount of money, you'll reinvest it into a different business.

When you have a plan, you have peace of mind, because having a plan set in your mind puts everything into a frame that allows you to act in alignment within that frame.

If you have a plan, you'll program your brain into finding solutions and going in the direction you want the business to be at the end. Without it, you're going to tread water heading in no direction.

TWENTY-THREE
TOTAL WEALTH MINDSET

Now let's step back into the space of discussing principles that can apply to the digital marketing industry but are also applicable to business of any kind.

I want to introduce a concept that changed my life. It's pretty simple, but it took me a while to internalize and embrace it in my life. Every time I thought I had it figured out, it turned out to have an extra layer or example from my day-to-day life.

This is based on, just like so many parts of this book, personal development seminars, real life experiences, my personal therapy, and my mental coaching sessions.

Total Wealth Mindset Lesson #1

A **wealth mindset** is when a person really, truly believes there's "enough for everyone to eat." Now, don't get me wrong, the fact that there's enough for everyone does not mean that getting that prey or that becoming that predator is easy. It's not. But this is the first lesson for a reason. Without this foundation, things are going to be more difficult later.

Someone with a wealth mindset believes:

- They will always have money, and clients will always want them.
- The next business partner or romantic relationship is just right around the corner.
- They truly deserve the good that this world has to offer.
- They are skillful enough to always land on their feet—regardless of whether a client leaves them, their romantic partner dumps them, or their business partner decides they want to change course and do something else.

Wealth-minded people would never try to convince someone (a business partner or a romantic partner) to stay with them, or even be angry at that person or themselves when someone decides to end the relationship. Why? Because they believe they can always find the right match, and that there will always be plenty of options.

I'm not talking about FOMO (fear of missing out). They don't go into any type of relationship looking to get out of it and search for the next best thing. It's not like they disrespect their partners because they have wealth—it's something more internal, a feeling that you deserve to live your best life, and because of that, you don't want or need anyone specific.

Money comes and money goes. Partners come and partners go. Even your parents and the people you love will one day no longer be there.

Everything bad that happened in my life, as bad as it felt when it happened, turned out for the best throughout the years. In hindsight, everything either made me stronger or created a situation where I grew mentally, personally, or financially to a better place and got more in life, business, or a relationship.

Did it feel horrible, dark, and death-like at the moment it happened? Of course, but looking back I can't remember something that didn't end up directing me towards a better life in some way.

This brings me directly to Lesson 2.

Total Wealth Mindset Lesson #2:

The language and choice of words we use in our day-to-day conversations and the talks we have with ourselves have a bigger impact than you might think.

Words create the way we view this world. Essentially, our perception of this world is generated by the words we use and the way we choose to tell ourselves and other people the story.

And since perception of reality, is reality => perception is reality.

So, if words = perception,

And perception = the way we view the world, our reality,

Then, words = reality.

This involves everything that happens in your life. If a campaign failed, or an account was banned, and you choose to describe it as a disaster and a catastrophe, that's how you're going to experience it.

For me, studying human design brought me to understand that the way I learned is by making mistakes. As someone who can be very self-flagellating, this self-knowledge helped me change the words in my story from "failures" and "mistakes" (those I've made in businesses and in my personal life, with friends or female partners I've had) to **"lessons."** Since I'm learning from these experiences, this helped me deal with and add closure to the difficulties I've been through.

Total Wealth Mindset Lesson #3

This is something we talked about earlier in this book: Don't combine one thing that happened to you with another thing, because in those cases 1+1=3 and not 2.

Align the belief that everything in life happens for a good reason with that total wealth mindset, and you should be able to better handle everything life or business throws at you. You really can.

I'm not saying it's not going to hurt, or you won't feel bad at times, I'm saying you're going to improve the way you bounce back and lessen the time and level to which you suffer.

Sure, it may take more time for the younger audience members that read this to create enough life experience to instill that certainty—to know that you can withstand certain situations in your business and in your life and overcome them time after time.

Making the shift into giving, as a part of embracing a total wealth mindset, is critical. Regardless of where you're coming from, if you go to an industry event with a "survival mindset" you're going to look for what things you can take, extract, and maximize from the situation. To some degree this is okay, but it could also create a feeling of discomfort at best, or inauthenticity/dishonesty at worst for the other person you're talking to, especially if they come from a different mindset.

Remember, the research shows white-hat, long-term thinking always overcomes black-hat, short-term thinking. Unless you're sure you're going to die in a couple of years, you're making a mistake by not playing the long game. And **giving**—whether it's knowledge, advice, a tip, or an introduction—**will always win in the long-term game**.

When I say white hat or black hat, I don't mean how "clean" your campaigns are or the niche that you are in; that's a small, technical part of it. I mean that when you are in a white hat mentality, you are looking to give, not waiting to get hurt, and not trying to "hit and run" by taking from people. You're not putting any energy into what others think of you or in concealing what you're making money from because that's a short-term mindset. That approach will only hold up for so long before it becomes disconnected from reality in many industries, but especially in the digital marketing industry.

Why is a miserly approach, black-hat mindset short-term thinking? Because you don't know what you're going to do, own, or need this year, next year, or in five years. You don't know where someone is going to be, own, or be able to give you this year, next year, or in five years. They might go get that knowledge from somewhere else, so why not be remembered as someone who has helped them?

Now, when I talk about giving, I'm not saying that you should let yourself be exploited or stop your life and business in order to give a stranger whatever they want, I trust you to have the common logic to make the right decision when it comes to it, all I want you to start with is knowing that you're probably not the smartest person in the room, if there's even someone like that, and that people see through it if you hide things or act in a manipulative way.

The only way I found to win every time is to change a selfish way of thinking during a conversation to "What can I give or how can I help this person?" That's much more in service than thinking "How can I/we make money together" or just focusing on what you want to get and the questions you came with to the conference. Building that small, initial relationship from a place of generosity also allows you to increase your chances of actually getting what you want from others later on in your career.

TWENTY-FOUR
THE INDUSTRY IS YOUR PLAYING FIELD FILLED WITH OPPORTUNITIES

I've had people say that their gut told them not to do business with someone, that all the warning signs were there. I've experienced this as well. They revealed private things on the first or second call that really made me feel bad, stressed, or pushed into the deal. They say bullying statements like: "This is what I pay, you need to decide *now* if you're taking it or not."

The biggest lesson I've learned is that when the energy isn't there, trust your gut and know that it's okay to say "no" or back away from the deal.

There are lots of deals, offers and potential partners out there for you, and some of these initial options that you're saying no to right now might come back later as better deals. Later, that person might understand you're harder to acquire, and that will give you much more flexibility and also potentially higher payouts or build a better name for yourself.

To be brutally honest, if you feel like you need to say "yes" to everything, that should be a strong enough sign that you need to work harder and create more opportunities for yourself.

I've known agencies where people told me for years how expensive they were, and what your minimum needed to be to get accepted as a client there. Without even knowing them or anyone who owns or works there, my own perception of them has been that they were good or even better than any other agency.

Saying no is a part of a being true to your brand and that long-term strategy I've been writing about throughout this book.

Next, we'll look at what happens when you go "all in" but your mindset doesn't match that strategy.

TWENTY-FIVE
THE VICIOUS CYCLE OF PLAYING "ALL IN"

Y ou can't be your true self when you're "all in" and until you have a full belief that you deserve everything you want—aka you've achieved the total wealth mindset.

What I mean by this is if you're always playing with everything you have, betting it all, AND you don't 100% believe in yourself and your abilities (that even if you lose it all you can create that same amount or even more wealth again), you're not going to make good decisions while playing.

Think about it. This can apply to any part of your life, such as with women or men, when you dated someone you *really* wanted to be with and part of you believed it would be tough to meet someone like that again, you weren't yourself. You were too afraid to lose, so you couldn't be authentic. Most often these imbalanced relationships fail, and you are left heartbroken and filled with regret.

But how do you escape that cycle? This is almost like telling someone, "You need experience to gain experience." Right? Because if you don't have success in business, and do not have a lot of money, you might not play "all in" and make bad, anxiety-driven, decisions.

It starts with full accountability.

You can't evolve without it.

I've had so many consultations when the person was continuously victimizing themselves and telling me the string of partners they've had in their lives and how they all did him wrong.

Here's a secret. *Every business or any other relationship you experience is a reflection of what you love and hate about yourself.*

It always takes two to tango, and at the end of the day, you are left with yourself.

The secret to discovering resilience is first to find the resistance you have in yourself, those patterns lurking inside you that lure you into negative thinking. To find those patterns you have to do two things:

1. Be curious
2. Approach it with no ego at all

What you resist = what persists.

And your patterns will continue to block or slow down your progress. If you can't be curious and non-judgmental about yourself and the inner obstacles you're facing, you will not be able to confront them so you can evolve and progress.

Go back to those moments where you felt things weren't working with partners or people you worked with and understand where you were wrong.

What we do too often is constantly repeat a certain story to ourselves and other people, campaigning until we believe that story, even if it's a lie. Usually, the first story or narrative we come up with is the one where we're the good guys or the victims.

But there is another storyline—the *whole* truth.

When we tell the first story, deep inside we know that's not the whole truth, and as we repeat it, we believe it more and more. However, when we learn to focus on what's actually true, or where we were wrong, we are able to improve ourselves and move forward. Until we do that, we're just going to create more and more of these same situations, and the same types of woe-is-me stories. They may feature different people or happen in different locations...but they're the same failures.

Remember, there's no point in telling that story to yourself or others—because the ONLY constant thing in those stories is **you**. The circumstances and people may change, but you can't fix or improve them, you can **only improve yourself**.

At the end of the day, if you have already lost something, or made a mistake, the only way to make it worthwhile is by taking full accountability and searching for your contribution to the loss. Discover what you can learn from it. What is the lesson here? Even if you were, indeed, a victim of circumstance, you still need to own your part. The more you change your mindset from victim to hunter, seeking out your patterns to change them, the greater the rewards you'll reap.

If you learn from difficulties you face, you turn a mistake (or even a disaster) into a learning experience, a lesson that helps with both changing how you look at life and learning how to judge yourself less. Meaning your past experiences might've been difficult, but once you've addressed them you can move into the future with renewed optimism and look forward to much better experiences.

That's the only way that I know how to manage disappointment without getting sucked into the mindset of victimhood and failure. This has been immensely effective for me in breaking these cycles and evolving in business and personally.

Next, we'll look at how to bring in your total wealth mindset and learning from past failures together into the art of negotiating a deal.

TWENTY-SIX

THE TWO SECRETS TO NEGOTIATING A DEAL

Whether we talk about a business you create with a potential partner, an affiliate offer you negotiate with a network or a direct advertiser, or even a small joint venture you're testing, make sure you are structuring the deal to fit you. This not only keeps you safe from potential issues that may arise in the future, it also increases the chances of that deal succeeding because you're going to tie up a lot of loose ends that might've been harder to fix once the business is already making money or work is continuing at a fast pace.

I'm going to share with you my two greatest secrets when it comes to negotiating a deal. They'll not only help you to maximize your profit and LTV within the deal, but also help you create more opportunities and longer-term clients.

The two secrets are my **"Fallback Strategy"** and the **"Exit Sign Rule."**

Let's start with the first one, the fallback strategy.

When I go into a deal—especially when I know I'm going into a meeting where there's a potential of the client firing me or wanting to renegotiate the situation—I always make sure that I have a fallback strategy. It's kind of like a down sell if I could compare it to the marketing world.

So, in these situations I will always consider exactly what my options are and what I'm going to do. That's what I call my fallback strategy.

However, a fallback strategy isn't enough. You need the second part, what I call the "exit sign" rule. The Exit Sign Rule is the willingness to leave at any given moment. This needs to be communicated in two ways—directly and indirectly, meaning you not only have to say this philosophy, but you also have to enact it.

Say you are on a call with the other party who might want to renegotiate terms. You can tell them, "I'm not telling you these points just to convince you to stay with our partnership," but then you lower your monthly retainer. Those two things are at cross-purposes. Another example is if you say, "I'm not going to try and convince you to change course," but later you offer a different option. These mixed signals will make you appear as if you're just using selling tactics—they don't come across as genuine.

In poker they say, "Never bluff without having outs," outs being even the slightest chance of winning the pot/money. Here I'll say you really need to embody the mindset of true wealth and be completely willing to give up on the deal, zero hesitation. That's the only way it's going to make an impact on the other person.

If you don't feel like you can let go of that client, their business, or a specific deal, it could turn out negatively in the long run, especially because it undermines an authentic wealth mindset.

To have "true wealth," you understand and believe that what's yours is yours, regardless of the current deal or opportunity in front of you at the moment. If this deal right now doesn't happen the way you believe it needs to happen, you know you're not missing anything—there will be other, better deals out there for you.

Sometimes I've had to act on what I said or implied and actually exit the deal because I didn't get the right equity or the terms I wanted. But believe me, if a deal is right for you, it'll come back to you, and that deal will arrive better than ever because you waited for it to become ideal and meet your standards. This ability to wait will allow that deal to come back around to put you in an even more amazing position. Again, this only works if you believe that it's completely okay if it doesn't work out in the end.

One more key point I want to mention here is that you should consider using this method beyond a situation where there's a negotiation or a change in the deal happening. If you want this approach to be effective, this attitude needs to be communicated right from the start.

I suggest you write some notes or bullet points that you can memorize for that meeting, just like you would study for a test in school. Even if you don't remember them all, you can bring up a few if that person surprises you with a situation where you need to negotiate.

Something I want to point out is that throughout my years of consulting, I've noticed some people go overboard with this concept by making a list of everything that the partner has ever done wrong. People think that this will be useful should they reach a stage in the relationship where they need to have a negotiation, so they can throw all those points in the other person's face. This is a mistake—this is not why you've created your list. This approach doesn't put you in a favorable position at all because it shows you're only focusing on all the negatives... which could cause that person to become defensive and trend toward less desirable traits even more.

Let me give you an example from personal experience:

Recently a client I had worked with for a year decided that I was too expensive for him. No one else in the company was on a rev share, and he could bring in a much cheaper person to manage his media budgets.

He told me that it didn't make sense to keep both media buyers for the company. He wanted to terminate my contract.

During the time we worked together, I knew he'd replaced his previous partner and fired people (some of whom never got paid), and I recognized he wasn't someone who stood by his word. I'd also seen him do the same thing to some affiliates, so I suspected he might pull a move like that on me.

So, I decided to prepare two sets of notes for our negotiation meeting.

The first set of notes was for a case where he tells me that our contract is invalid, and he refuses to even pay for the last two months I've worked for him—meaning he won't respect the three months' notice he has to give me that's in our contract. The second set of notes spoke to a scenario where the call would be much fairer, and I would be able to offer him a fallback solution.

This place of "tough negotiation tactics" isn't where I like to be since I planned to only respond to whatever he would say. He could have surprised me with something else, and in general I like being the person that leads the moves, but I couldn't foresee his reasons so I prepared the best I could.

Luckily for me (and him) the call went the second way, and I was able to pull off a fallback.

I gave him five examples of things I had contributed for the company that the new team could not have done, and I made sure he understood that these things happened in the past, meaning that while he might've fixed those problems earlier, the issues persisted. I wasn't confident the new team would understand how to control the same scenarios in which I was able to help him regain control.

I began by telling him that I didn't want to stay if he didn't want me to, and I wasn't going to try to convince him to keep me, but there are some things to consider. For instance, the fact that he does not know his reps on the media buying platforms and does not have connections with the policy people I have.

My comments prompted him to ask me what I thought he

should do. I told him I also offer a consulting service for a much lower price than what he was paying me, so if he hired me as a consultant, I would not do the day-to-day work I was doing at the time, but I'd be happy to help him keep in touch with those reps, etc. He ended up paying me the three months' "buy out" of the contract plus accepting that consultation retainer.

If I did not have that fallback strategy and hadn't stated my case in a way in which I was also willing to give up on him as a client (which I was, truly), he would never have kept me. My approach was something that had to be done in that specific moment and during that particular conversation. You have to consider all angles and know what planned approaches are right for you.

This is also true when dealing with direct advertisers or networks. Maybe they're going to say the traffic isn't good, or that you need to lower caps (daily amount of leads/sales you're sending right now). Do you have a specific plan in mind?

Do they know that you're willing to leave and pause (even winning) campaigns at any given moment? Are you willing to go "all in" on that strategy and pause one winning campaign so that they know that you mean business?

Weight your options and plan your talking points before you engage in conversations of negotiation.

TWENTY-SEVEN
CREATE PARTNERSHIPS, NOT EMPLOYEES

I remember when I was building my first agency, I had an older partner who was in the advertising world before me. He told me "Employees are here to take what they can from you and fuck you up. You'll need to recruit a large number of them to find really good ones who stick with you," and he was right, most of them are.

Throughout time I saw a massive number of mistakes that were made by people's employees.

I could not tell you the amount of money I have made due to unqualified people working for other companies, with and without intention on their side and mine.

It was at that point in time where I decided that I'm going to try to scale through partnerships.

Of course, there are certain types of businesses that just need to have employees in order to function, my fitness center being one of them.

But if you build it the right way—get rid of tasks that take up too much time and don't bring clear benefits when you do them yourself, especially repetitive work that can make you feel exhausted—and concentrate on areas where you can make a real difference, while also stepping back when the business can run on its own, then you'll have a great strategy in place. One that not only helps people and also generates more time for you, but also helps you expand and diversify. This means you are not only generating more cash and helping people around you, but you are also generating more time for yourself.

My formula when it comes to business structures:

- Do most of the stuff by yourself at the beginning.
- Only add cheap labor for what I call the "copy-paste" work that you add 0 value to when doing it yourself.
- Add partners who will take equity in order to scale or develop systems, and make sure that you have partners who are managing employees and affiliates.
- Stay active in the business as long as you have to, when you don't - set up a new one and keep the older one running.

People tend to ask me how I created a situation where I have all these businesses without working a lot of hours, so here's an example of how to diversify your time and money to not only create stabilization but also to create more time:

1. Recognize the types of people you can really trust and test the relationship over time.
2. Build a team around them and make sure they are able to make day-to-day decisions without consulting and being dependent on you.
3. Make sure they have equity in the business, sometimes even much more than you. It's also worth mentioning that if you're not going to play an active part in the business, then you probably want to make sure you have less than 20%, regardless of how much money you're going to put inside.

By using this method, you're going to build teams that do not rely on you, and people who do not look at the business as employees, but as partners. They are going to work harder, be more open to hearing about different ideas, work longer hours if needed, and treat the place as their own, because it is.

There is just nothing more powerful than an employee that owns a small part of the business.

While I do give out equity, I always make sure that this person knows it's contingent on them keeping up a certain level of work, and they know I can take away that equity at any time if they don't. That part was always "written in blood" because people got comfortable when the business started making money and either stopped working or added people below them to do the job.

Over the first months / years, when the business needs more of my time, I'll be a lot more involved, and when the business takes off – I'll leave it to open up and expand with more businesses. That way I'm not dependent on one business or industry and I "duplicate" my time so that my businesses are growing even when I'm not around or actively growing them.

When do I take on teams and recruit? Whenever I need a particular position to be manned all the time, I need to complete "copy-paste" types of jobs, or when there's stuff that doesn't require my specific brain to make a dynamic decision. This would be stuff like:

- Answering messages online,
- Setting up appointments,
- Creating creatives, and
- Uploading campaigns that need to be uploaded in a specific way.

Actually, campaigns are a very good example on how I separate the two types of scenarios in which I need to either do it myself or use my team to do it.

If it's a brand-new campaign or a new product, I don't know

if it's going to be profitable or what's the right platform / campaign structure to run it. In that situation, I'll probably try to run it myself at first. But if that campaign is already running and I'm looking to scale it, if I don't have time available, I can use my team to do it for me.

The concept of "getting a team" has been abused by gurus and the fake mentality.

Every 21-year-old kid has an assistant and a team behind them.

When I see it, I honestly see it as fake because I'm like, dude, you're 21, where's the hustle? How fast could you have grown that you can't handle it yourself at this moment? And if you did - was growing that fast healthy?

For me, it tells me that the person is more into looking good in front of other people than actually working and hustling, but I might just be getting old.

TWENTY-EIGHT
THE REALITY IS: RELATIONSHIPS END

I once heard a sentence that made me laugh: "Partnerships usually change when people make too much money or not enough money."

It's funny, but often also true, whether we talk about a partnership or any type of other relationship—between you as an agency and a client, between you as an affiliate and the network or even the direct advertiser you are working with, things could escalate.

Fighting, negotiating, and sometimes cutting relationships are a part of it all, and while as trivial as it sounds, some people expect all relationships to last forever.

People change, margins change, and especially in an industry like the affiliate/digital marketing industry, these things happen all the time, so expect them to be extra-dynamic.

As easy and simple as it may sound, yes, relationships end, most of the time—and that's okay and a part of the game. I'm not saying this should mean you need to act on cutting those relationships faster and I'm not trying to say you shouldn't get into one just because it'll end sometime.

I'm saying it because of two things:

1. People feel amazed and tend to burnout quicker when they experience an ending of a relationship - a client, network, campaign, partnership, or an advertiser decides to cut the relationship, I even saw some people change (go crazy almost) to the point where I didn't recognize them.
2. When it happens, sometimes people would try to hold on to them, by convincing them, by offering different things - and this just does not work in the long run.

Managing a situation where you are pushed or have placed yourself in a corner aka what I call "last call" situations, when you're essentially screwed, is something that I hope you do not experience, but you do need to have it in your arsenal.

I had been contacted by an advertising company owner that didn't have a digital agency and wasn't giving any digital services.

We decided to set up that part of his business together and split the profits 50%-50% between us.

That company was supposed to be fed the advertising company's clients, but was supposed to be opened as a separate entity, the operation started making a lot of money pretty quick and we decided to start drafting a contract between us so that we would form the company officially, the contract started dragging on, and I finally realized I was getting fucked, the contract was never going to be signed, I was given excuses on where and why the lawyer didn't answer me, and I realized I had two options:

1. Get out of the business relationship and leave whatever I had created back there.
2. Drag it out for as long as I could, collect evidence of what was going on, and sue at the end.

I decided to go with #2 because I didn't want any future business relationship with those people anyway, so I didn't mind burning bridges.

I'm going to say something hard, but true. There are certain situations in life where life is worthless, like in wars or in certain countries. You can't behave the same as you normally would, and you can't expect to be treated according to certain rules of conduct...not when the location, amount of money at stake, or the situation has changed. In those circumstances, it's okay to make the decision to kill the partnership. But remember, you need to be prepared to be treated differently when certain things change.

That company would have been formed if certain things had gone differently, and maybe if the company had made less money, or had taken longer to make money. Those, as well as other elements in that deal changed how much it was worth to them to fuck me over and get me out of the company.

The day had come, the main partner called me and said he's getting one of his family members in the company to take over and that he's telling me goodbye, he also knew that I knew it all along.

Learning their plans, realizing that I was getting screwed, and understanding that I was naive to a certain extent helped me get more out of the lame situation that I was in.

Was it smart getting myself into that situation in the first place? *No.*

Was it smart to go to war with them? *Maybe.*

You are going to make mistakes. You are going to get into tough spots. If not, you're not learning, and you're not progressing at the pace you need to. Sometimes the best you can do is to manage losses and learn how to maximize even that kind of situation.

TWENTY-NINE
DEALING WITH TERRITORIAL PEOPLE, NEGATIVE FEEDBACK, AND ARGUMENTS

t doesn't really matter if you're an affiliate, an agency, or a brand trying to work with agencies on getting traffic, you are going to encounter some territorial people throughout your career, that's just a fact. They might be getting paid a lot and want to protect their environment; they might see your agency as someone who could replace them, and they might just want to look better/smarter than you.

Here's how to recognize them:

- They act based on survivalism - you'll get the feeling that they don't believe there's enough for everyone to eat.
- They'll prioritize whatever makes them look good internally within the company.
- They love being followed and having followers around them.
- They dislike leaders or anyone who has something creative to say that doesn't follow the exact line they were thinking.

You can see how this would cloud their judgment—they might go so far as to lose money or the company's money just to make you lose money or your position as an affiliate/agency inside the company, or even just to prove you wrong or to make themselves look better or advance their position.

The thing about these people is that they tend to be repetitive, meaning they'll continue with this pattern, going from one person to another, villainizing them one by one. They simply cannot control their behavior, it's stronger than they are.

They are usually also pathological liars, it's a part of their nature to lie—about everything.

The most effective way I've found for dealing with them is to:

1. Bever call them out on it, especially not in front of people. There's absolutely no point in that.
2. Only react when you have to stand your ground—for example when you try to answer, and that person won't let you finish talking.
3. Make sure you point out certain undebatable things they do that do not benefit the company. For example, I was in a situation where I was missing something related to tracking inside a campaign we were setting up, and that person kept telling the company's owners that he knew that I missed something, and I was trying to run a campaign and spending the company's money when it was never going to work with this issue.

I immediately pointed out to the owners of the company that this was not just a non-team player move, it was also counter intuitive towards the company's benefit, as the company was not only not making money, but was actually losing. Clearly. he knew that and it was more important for him to show that I wasn't as good as they thought, even at the expense of losing money.

This employee firmly believes he deserves wealth and insists that he would never have acted this way once the company became successful, point blank.

That's a very hard statement to deal with, even if you're a master at debates.

In the long run, as long as you keep the cold war under the radar, a good company CEO would either put an end to the toxic relationship with the employee, or separate that employee from the company and turn them into a service provider.

Having said that, there are lots of times when it's going to take time for people to understand you are right and appreciate the fact that you pointed out reality; this person will make more mistakes just like that, and in the next times he does, whatever you pointed out in the past will be linked to it and a pattern will be recognized.

Once recognizing this sort of person, I suggest going one of two ways:

1. Either make them your best friend and control the situation, trying to defuse them in that way. I like this method because it's a more peaceful one.
2. Sever any connection to them. Even your own internal thoughts about them need to be positive, as if you have never met them. This takes practice and only works when you are really done with trying to win against them / campaign against them etc.

What do you do when someone gives you bad feedback regardless of whether they are a territorial person or not? Negative feedback will always happen. For example it could be something that's just plain and simple, like that your conversation rate is low, or that the leads you are selling to them are bad. It could also be how they interpret things like a bad joke or something they see as your bad behavior, of you personally, of something you did at an event, or something they noticed while working with you. Whether it's personal or technical, the best way to deal with it consists of two things:

1. First, thank them for letting you know.
2. Then, let them know you understand what they mean and it's great that they've told you.

Most people in that situation would defend their position, and their response would usually be:

- Showing that person why he's wrong and explaining themselves.
- Trying to hurt that person back by saying something hurtful too.
- Or my favorite one, the infantile response of saying "well you're doing it too" or "you did it first." This sounds too much like "he started it, Mom," doesn't it?

These are all responses that don't resolve the conflict, and they also leave the other person stuck in the same belief and digging into their perception of you.

It's quite simple logic:

If that person is wrong, then he's an idiot who would never understand what you're trying to explain to him anyway, and you should tell him he's right because you just can't teach a donkey.

If that person is right, then you should tell him he's right, because why not?

Regardless, remember two important things that need to remain on the top of your mind throughout any argument or simply when you're dealing with people:

1. You do not possess "the truth" or "all the truth."
   People see things differently and perception of reality

is reality. Even though you might be certain of what you see and how you see things, there must be even a grain of truth to what they are saying, and even if not, in order for you to get ahead, you need to understand where they are coming from.

2. When you tell someone that they are right and thank them for letting you know, make sure that you say it authentically. There's a fine line between successfully using this method and sounding sarcastic so it backfires on you.

When you're trying to get your point across and give some feedback to the other side, make sure you start by listening to the other side and letting them know they are being heard. You can do this by doing two things:

1. Reflecting back what they said. Usually when you do this, they respond with some "adjustments" or "fine-tuning" of what they said, and the normal response would be to reflect that back to them. That doesn't mean repeating exactly what they said, but yes, make sure they understand that they are being heard.

2. Labeling and giving small disclaimers to what you're going to say. Labeling means that when a person says something, you reflect that back to him, and you can start labeling it by saying "it sounds like," "it must feel like," or "I hear what you're saying that...." When you use these phrases, not only does that person feel like he's heard, but he also feels understood, which defuses a lot of negative outcomes.

Disclaimers are used in situations when you're about to say something bad or negative, or you're just criticizing what the other person is saying. For example, you could say something like "I don't think you're going to like what I'm going to say now," or "You're going to hate me after I say this, but I still have to say it." Usually that person would think what you said isn't that bad. Providing a disclaimer also defuses negative feedback or rejection on the other side.

THIRTY
RULES OF THE GAME

The basic rules of the business game are very simple:

1. Create as much money as possible.
2. Hold on to that money for as long as possible.
3. Invest that money when possible.
4. Spend as little as possible.

When people get into the day-to-day of managing a business, they tend to forget about the basic rules and deviate from the course that's supposed to take them there. Alternately, they take on bigger risks where the ratio between the investments they are putting down—cash or time—and the chances of that business making money is really bad.

Common mistakes I've seen are:

1. Someone opens a business and the first thing they do is tell everyone, each day, that they are a business owner, by posting online about it, buying a luxury car, or by investing too much time in PR related stuff.

These people are usually in the "looking good" business and not any other business.

2. Someone hires more people as soon as they make a profit regardless of how much they really need them. People like these are addicted to managing people and ignore the basic rule about spending as little as possible. Maybe they're replacing it with "making the business as big as I can."

I was talking to a friend who told me, "His company is big" and "That guy's company is so amazing and has hundreds of employees." Keep reminding yourself that it's not about how big your company is or how many employees you have. Small companies can make a lot of money, and big companies can lose a lot of money. Size doesn't matter.

I'm seeing people in the industry that I always joke about how much they don't like making money. At the first opportunity, they get more employees, better offices, and dream about a long-term business, while in reality, they could or should:

1. Save more money for when the business or industry goes down, or just when they take a hit.
2. Make more money with a smaller team by investing in better technology and automation.

Some people keep going through the cycle of:

Making money > getting more employees > understanding that they have too many employees > moving into a narrower company structure.

The number of people who make this mistake is huge, so it's important to keep reminding yourself of the basic rules of the game.

The main thing to keep in mind throughout your journey is to use common sense: when talking to other people, when listening to others, when choosing a potential partner, and when negotiating salaries and payouts.

Using common sense and asking yourself questions when things don't make sense could keep you from making more mistakes and potentially losing more money than you would.

Set up a target, create value by offering a solution, whether with or without a team or a service, that helps with something.

Set up milestones: in cash, number of clients, or subscriptions. Create a specific plan that you understand that is simple to manage and change if needed. All along the way, use common sense and keep asking yourself the following question about every decision you're making: "Is this getting me close to or keeping me away from my goals and milestones?"

Yes, at the beginning it's going to feel weird asking yourself that question.

And yes, it's going to be hard remembering to ask that question every time.

But just like when you start a workout routine, with time and consistency this will become a habit. I don't think you need to have more than two rules/habits in place at the beginning. The core two are:

1. **Being goal oriented**: Ask yourself with every conversation or situation what you want to achieve or gain from it, even when the action you're taking is to give something.
2. **Applying common sense**: Ask yourself questions: Is this person telling a lie? Is this realistic? Is this action bringing me closer to my goals or not?

Once you've got these questions ingrained in your daily routine and thought process during a conversion, your life will be much easier. Will this give you a faster track on achieving your goals? YES! This works like a charm, for anyone and every time.

Once understanding, living, and acting by these basic rules, we can start adding more stuff like:

1. Learning through different channels.
2. Recruiting other people.
3. Impacting others.
4. Sharing with others.

These are all great tools of expanding yourself, implementing a "total wealth mindset" into your life and really understand that by giving, you receive much more and that it is your interest at the end of the day to be surrounded by people who are as successful as possible, not because of how you look on the outside, but because this directly helps you get more.

THIRTY-ONE
ONE INDUSTRY, DIFFERENT SIDES

n 2021 I was invited to speak at an Amazon conference in Orlando. It wasn't a big event, as Amazon masterminds usually are. I was speaking on the second day and had the chance to hear some of the other speakers.

Most audience members were people who just sell on Amazon. I was hearing some of the other speakers talk about "Affiliate Marketing 101," like, really basic stuff. The Amazon audience was amazed by run-of-the-mill Shopify features. The idea of monetizing data like emails and SMS wowed them. Then, one speaker talked about using the "exit traffic" to generate more profit from the same traffic by sending them to third party affiliate offers and then explained how to choose them. Everyone's jaws dropped and their eyes opened wide.

Me and this other speaker who has a similar background to mine were joking about how old that knowledge and those methods are, and I said to him, "I can't believe that most of these people don't have a clue about what he's saying." The other speaker explained to me that there are different aspects of this industry. Affiliates don't know or want to deal with inventory, networks usually don't want to deal with buying traffic, Amazon people don't know much about things outside of the

Amazon and retail space, and brand owners usually use agencies to do their job for them. Of course, that changes between countries, brands, industries, and specific products, but in general, the percentage of people who grasp all these aspects is small, very small. And that's ok, that's how collaborations and opportunities thrive and come about.

That small percentage—those "jack of all trades" people—in my opinion, should really be embracing diversification. The digital marketing space is probably the most diversified industry out there (or at least as far as I know). So, if you're able to understand how design, code, payment processing, Shopify apps, API, and media buying work, even just a bit, you'll be able to communicate better with colleagues and team-mates. Let's face it, there's a big chance of someone tricking you into some time-wasting, money-draining dumpster fire of a project that's never going to succeed.

And the biggest thing about it is that if you're always open to the next thing, not being able to learn in-depth knowledge, you're sort of walking a tightrope without a safety net. It's like always going "all in" on the first hand you're dealt at a poker game. You might win here and there, but the odds are stacked against you. I keep seeing too many people do this in business. They might be masters of Facebook ads or they're great at opening and managing an agency. But what happens to them when Facebook goes down? Or when there's a new traffic source? They've sunk everything into branding themselves at that one thing, and probably invested a lot of their time into a certain community, working on a certain platform.

I just don't see it as a smart move when you can still learn new traffic sources, learn how to be less dependent on a graphic designer or a coder. This allows you to:

1. Move faster.
2. Open up your mind to new ideas.

3. Be more creative inside your current project and when thinking about new projects.
4. Check the quality of the work you are getting.
5. Communicate better with the people who work with/for you.
6. Be open to creating automations that can save you a lot of time and money.

And again, I'm not suggesting you attend a 3-year designing or coding school, but I do think you need to understand the basics. At the very least you should understand the terminology and how to work with certain products your team uses.

After you finish reading this book, I hope you'll see the fact that a wide range of roles exist in the industry is an opportunity. Why? Because, for someone who is good at either media buying or building funnels, connecting with someone from the Amazon industry who is a master of manufacturing, fulfillment, shipping, and customer service could be the perfect match for you.

Don't look at something you do not know or understand as weird or scary, but as a place where you can thrive and gain an advantage. If there's anything you should take from this book when it comes to opportunities, it's this: You do not have to do the whole 360. Connect with people you believe have good products and whom you trust and start building something together!

THIRTY-TWO
THERE'S ALWAYS MORE MONEY TO BE MADE

You know how they say that the social media platform's algorithm recognizes what you like and shows you more of it? Like, if you're right wing, you're much likely to see more right-wing political stuff, Or, if you love a certain TV show, you'll probably see more posts about it. We all know how that works on paid ads and also on organic posts, and as marketers, we understand it. That's a really good way of increasing our time on the site and it's in direct correlation with the money that the platforms make.

The problem is, just like in social media, life has a way of attracting the same types of opinions and people to us. This means that when things aren't working, we'll hear more people say that it's not possible to make money anymore: "the agency model is broken," "the hay days are gone," "CPMs are too high," and/or "affiliate marketing is dead."

But at the end of the day, there's money all around us, and people are still generating it all the time. That's a big point you have to keep in your head all the time because when you lose at certain projects and campaigns, you're going to start making up reasons for it, and all of those quotes I just wrote (and more) are going to come up fast.

It's important not to get sucked into a conversation that only gives excuses about why things aren't working for you right now and why you are right and shouldn't be blamed.

I had a partner named Nikola, a very smart person who was very pessimistic and afraid on one hand, but also said some very optimistic things. One of those things turned into the "Nikola Test" for me, kind of like a "reality check" for when you are either having a "dry season" or when things are not working out for you.

The Nikola test goes like this, you recognize that you are questioning yourself and or the project you are currently working on, step out of that situation and ask yourself:

1. Is anyone else successfully doing what I want to do right now? Is it possible or is there a big unfair advantage they have, and I don't?
2. Am I married to this idea? Should I divorce it and try to find something else that would create money?

The final answer is - if someone else is making it work, you can make it work too, as long as you know most of the reasons for why it's working for them.

It's a bit tricky because sometimes we'll ask ourselves the first question: is anyone else doing it? And the answer would be yes, but if it's Kim Kardashian's skin care product, or a company that has been around for 10-15 years, so it's important to ask yourself the second question: am I comparing myself to others in the same situation?

For example, if you know that the main reason a product succeeded was the initial investment made into its launch and creatives, you either have to come up with a way to get that cash or a way to get that result with no cash, or simply of another idea that doesn't require what you don't have right now.

You can't compare yourself as a brand-new skin care brand to l'Occitane and say that just because they're doing it so can you. If you are a marketer, look at what other marketers are doing. If you can't get the initial cash, get a partner who can. If you can't get a partner who has this ability, then partner with a big influencer in the space.

I want to say that the fact that other people might be doing it successfully doesn't mean that it's possible now, and it doesn't mean that it's possible with the resources you have right now. It's okay to dream, it's perfect that you're taking action, but you also have to be realistic and align your plans with reality, even if that means that you need to create those resources or delay this project in favor of something else, so you'll have those resources later on.

Another big thing to remember when researching whatever is working is the definition of "what's something that is working." Many people would use spy tools or the Facebook ad library and look at ads that are running, but just because something is running it doesn't mean it's working, it doesn't mean that it's profitable and it doesn't mean it's going to work for you.

Some companies are running ads while losing money, some are losing online to generate brand impressions and get more retail sales, some have just launched the campaigns that are losing, and it takes them time to optimize—if they'll ever be in the green—and some of them have a backend that's much stronger than the initial offer on the front end.

Keep in mind, looking at the ad is just the first step in research. You have to get creative.

For example, I once connected to people on LinkedIn who worked at a certain company—or former employees of that company—just to learn more about what they did and to create those connections.

When I look at those people online and at conferences who are "crying" about how nothing is working out for them I don't see them as losers. I have a lot of empathy for them because I was there once in my life, and I didn't have the tools to see what

I'm seeing now. This is just one scenario, and this is a story they're telling themselves inside their heads, and it's impacting not only how they view the world but also how they take actions and react to different scenarios.

THIRTY-THREE

WALKING THE LINE
BETWEEN BEING FEARED
AND BEING LIKED

The spectrum between being feared and being liked is something I've been interested in for at least the past ten years.

I first became interested in it when I was expecting to see a direct correlation between how liked my dad was and the money we had or his financial success. He was a guy everyone said hello to and liked when he walked down the street, but there were months where he wasn't bringing in any money.

That's when I really started digging into it, understanding the line between being feared and liked, and where exactly I want to be in order to maximize my financial profits. I'm not saying this is the only "line" or playground you will play in; it's one of many. But this is definitely something I noticed you have put a lot of weight into. Not only does it impact whether or not you're getting clients and work, but it also impacts your positioning in a deal.

If you create too much fear, people don't want to work with you. If you become too liked or likable, people want to be your friends but not to work with you. Or worse, they want to work with you because they think they'll have the upper hand when they need to negotiate pricing or ask you for stuff that's not included in the contract for example.

Just like in the wild, the way to reach the top of the food chain in this industry without cannibalizing your career or connections, or even worse, ending up as someone else's prey, is by finding the right balance. It's key for maintaining not just a business relationship but, I would even say, a friendship. Now when I say, "being feared," I'm not saying you should be so unpredictable that your friend or partner can't guess what you'll do next or to what levels you'll go to when you go crazy. I mean the right kind of respect-inspiring fear.

For example, be someone who acts on what he says, someone who's willing to step out of the relationship if needed. Don't be someone who just talks, be someone who also takes action.

Regarding that, in life, there are three types of people or performers: the first one is someone who makes a lot of noise about what he's going to do without really doing anything. The second type is someone who does what he says he'll do most of the time. The third and highest type of performer, and I would even say authenticity, is those who barely say anything; everyone knows and fears their next move - and they just do.

If you do manage to find the right balance of fear and likability, that will create the level of respect you need, in order to be in the perfect position when you want to make any move on one hand, and when protecting your position on the other hand.

THIRTY-FOUR
CONTINUOUSLY WINNING

I learned how to keep winning because of my obsession with stability. I kept seeing these "shooting stars" (people who were rockstars one day, everyone was talking about them, they were on all of the stages, affiliate networks were talking about how much money they'd made with them), only to find the next day that everything they had was gone, *they were gone.*

Their meteoric rise and subsequent catastrophic fall made me want to learn from their mistakes so that I wouldn't end up failing or face the same scary changes they went through. I wanted to do it better. That was the only way I could move closer to the stability I craved.

During my observations, I discovered there were usually two recurring themes to their failure:

Failure Theme 1:
Being dazzled by "celebrations." Meaning, they got lured into the affiliate lifestyle. They got sucked into partying too much, doing a lot of drugs, and not focusing on what made them win in the first place. They started traveling too much, spending

time with the wrong people, or hooking up with romantic partners who only used them for their money.

Some of them reached an amount of money that either made them too scared of trying to get more because they were afraid of losing—or afraid of everyone else talking about how they lost.

Real, consistent winners and true professionals do not care when people talk good or bad about them. Sure, it's nice or bad to hear it for a second, and sometimes you get dragged into it, but constant winners do not focus on what people are saying about them for more than a few moments because they are so obsessed with the next goal, even if they just achieved their current goal. They usually celebrate with themselves, and not for long.

Failure Theme 2:

Not building any "forward momentum." Forward momentum is huge. Those who don't create forward momentum usually falter when they are extremely successful in an area that works for them—either a funnel, an offer, or a niche—and they stick to only that method. They put everything they have into it, night and day, and they do not build anything else for their future, such as a business, a partnership, or just meeting new people. Everything revolves around what they are currently doing. When that happens, the brain creates tunnel vision, and even when they go to a conference, they look for people who are into that same niche. *They don't diversify.*

Like they teach in the first month of business school, a certain percentage (and not a small one) of the revenue of any business needs to go back to advertising. That's why you see already successful companies like Coca-Cola still advertising. In this industry, you need to invest time back into the business, not just money. Meaning you always have plans, a future relationship you want to create, or a project you pursue "on the side" (slowly) until you need to invest more time into it, and you know it's time to expand your focus. That has been a key part of why I manage to continuously win and create much higher stability.

When things come crashing down, and that may be inevitable at some point, whether someone was out of it because they were partying too much or because they lacked forward momentum, they're going to find themselves in a situation where their imposter syndrome is overwhelming. People saw them as winners, and they couldn't tell them the truth about their failures and risk looking bad. Or they become so impatient to get the new business going that it creates either a very high frustration or a disconnection from reality...or both...and they just fade away.

Always have plans for the future and several strategies to get you there. Always work on something new. Always plan to scale. Every business that doesn't grow ends up dying. And that's the ultimate prey move to avoid at all costs.

THIRTY-FIVE
TAKEAWAYS AND FINAL THOUGHTS

No matter what your age, we all have at least one thing we've accomplished that we never thought we could do.

If I could go back and meet my 18-year-old self, I'd see:

- Me with zero friends
- Me with less than $1,000 in his bank account
- Me with no support (financially or personally) from family
- Me with no inheritance or family business to go into
- Me with no teachers beyond what information I found on the internet
- Me with no experience with romantic relationships and none in sight

That 18-year-old boy had to run to the bathroom in high school during breaks because he didn't want anyone to know he had no one to talk to.

That boy was afraid of the upcoming weekend because he knew everyone was going out, and he didn't have anyone to call and ask if he could join.

That boy had to settle for being close friends with girls because he didn't believe he was worth anyone having a relationship with.

I wish I could tell him that *in just three years*, he would be able to save his parents from going bankrupt. In three years, he'd become a millionaire and go on to become one of the best at what he does.

I would tell him that in only three years, his whole life would change in every aspect.

I would tell him that those cool and popular kids in high school end up living the most boring lives—while he's going to live free, travel, meet people from across the globe, and do whatever he wants. And most of those kids will envy *him*.

He'll go on to buy a lavish penthouse in one of the most expensive cities in the world. He'll go on to date amazing, beautiful women. He'll have friends from around the world who show up for him whenever he lands somewhere... And he'll write a freaking book about it!

And if there's one thing I hope you'll take from these personal stories, whether you relate to all or some of them, is that it only takes one good opportunity. That good opportunity could come earlier or a little later in life. I know people who made it after they turned 50 years old, while others made it at 17.

The fact that you are still on your way does not mean you're lost. Comparing yourself to others, or even feeling a little jealous of someone, may be slightly inevitable along the way, but it's so important not to let it control you. Allow those thoughts to come into your mind and then pass. **The only way you lose this game is by letting thoughts of envy or jealousy control you...and then quitting.**

I hope that my promise of changing the way you look at certain aspects of your business, or your soon-to-be business, has encouraged you throughout this book. For some, this upgraded mentality should take you from your beginner's mindset and escalate you to the top of the food chain. For others, it might have prevented them from being an easy target or prey.

Those positive outcomes are an ongoing theme throughout this book, and that's why this book is for everyone, regardless of your position, how long you've been in business, or your salary. It's about understanding that there's always a "next level" and a "next stage." Sitting in a dark place with big dreams inside you is something that everyone goes through, likely several times during your life (if you're lucky it's only a few). With the helpful tips I offered you here, you should be able to start making those changes and understand that it can take four to five years for a person to completely change their life. But believe me—the outcome is completely worth it.

- It starts with letting go of the past.
- Moves into creating new goals and changing your mindset.
- Comes into the world of making big moves, despite your deep-down fears, and embracing the wealth mindset.
- And finally, understanding that there's no end point— it's a continuous journey called life; there is no set finish line.

It's about understanding what's real, what's possible, and what's fake, especially when every year the competition gets steeper.

It's about letting go of any investment in how people look at you and the stories you hear about yourself, because you recognize that people are going to have something to say about you regardless of what you do.

It's about understanding that there's no one direction or way to start (or restart). You have to create your own path by understanding what you like, what your unfair advantages are, and how to use them.

It's about connecting the dots—meaning, it's more than just talking the talk. You have to have passion, be smart enough to listen and make adjustments as you go and be able to push forward throughout this roller coaster ride of digital marketing, business, and life.

It's about pushing through that nerve-racking fear whenever you are about to break new ground and push into new realms.

It's about acknowledging the fact that you do not know everything, that you have blind spots. And you never treat anyone as if they are beneath you...while at the same time knowing how and when to ask for help.

If you see me at a conference and this book has had any sort of impact on you, or you want to share if this book had an impact on your career, please approach me and tell me about your experience, or send me a message on any of the platforms (YouTube (@wolfmaor) / Instagram / Facebook - @maorbn). I'd love to hear your story.

This book has meant so much to me, to share my experience and wisdom, and it would simply make me happy to know I had an impact on another person's life, company, or career.

ABOUT THE AUTHOR

Maor Benaim is a seasoned digital marketing professional and businessman who started his first business at age 12. Maor has been in the digital marketing space since 2010 and has years of experience in the industry. As a full-stack media buyer, he successfully managed his own investments while also developing innovative media buying methods across various platforms. His extensive knowledge and hands-on approach have made him a trusted name in the field.

Maor Benaim's expertise extends beyond personal success. As the founder of two thriving media agencies and over 10 brands, encompassing both Direct to Consumer (DTC) and brick and mortar, including a chain of fitness centers, his influence extends well beyond financial gains as demonstrated by the accolades he's received from industry peers and organizations.

In addition to his digital marketing ventures, Maor has been a dynamic public speaker since 2017. With years of experience, he has captivated audiences with his insights into the ever-evolving world of digital marketing and entrepreneurship. His ability to convey complex concepts with clarity and genuine enthusiasm has established him as a sought-after speaker at conferences and events worldwide.

"Unleashing Your Inner Wolf" is a testament to Maor's unwavering commitment to helping others navigate the intricacies of entrepreneurship, digital marketing, and achieving personal success. With his book, he not only imparts his professional wisdom but also shares his passion for helping others unlock their potential in the business world.

For more insightful content and practical advice from Maor Benaim, visit his YouTube channel: YouTube.com/@wolfmaor.

www.ingramcontent.com/pod-product-compliance
Lightning Source LLC
LaVergne TN
LVHW052023080426
835513LV00018B/2123